Cold Comfort

ung separated refugees in England

Kate Stanley

Save the Children

Save the Children is the UK's leading international children's charity. Working in more than 70 countries, it runs emergency relief alongside long-term development and prevention work to help children, their families and communities to be self-sufficient.

Drawing on this practical experience, Save the Children also seeks to influence policy and practice to achieve lasting benefits for children within their communities. In all its work, Save the Children endeavours to make children's rights a reality.

Published by
Save the Children
17 Grove Lane
London SE5 8RD
UK
Tel: (0) 20 7703 5400
Fax: (0) 20 7708 2508
www.savethechildren.org.uk

Published 2001
© The Save the Children Fund 2001
Registered Charity No. 213890

Foreword

Young people who come to England alone as refugees face a bewildering situation. Many are suffering from traumatic experiences. They are cut off from their families. They may have little knowledge of English.

It is estimated that there are more than 6,000 young people currently living in the UK who have come here alone and have sought asylum. This report is based on interviews carried out between July 2000 and February 2001 with 125 young separated refugees, as well as interviews with social workers, teachers and other professionals.

Once in England, the support and care on offer to these vulnerable young people is often shamefully inadequate. On the following pages, young people talk of being dumped in appalling and unsuitable accommodation, of being moved hundreds of miles from the local authority responsible for them, and of suffering bullying and racial attacks.

The research shows clearly that service provision for young separated refugees is uneven, inadequate and often uncoordinated. Resources are stretched, and there is frequently a lack of infrastructure and procedures for support. Some of the professionals interviewed readily acknowledged that young refugees receive a far worse service than indigenous children.

Save the Children is therefore calling on central government, local authorities and other agencies urgently to address the shortcomings highlighted in this report and to adopt a 'joined-up' approach in responding to the education, accommodation, health and social needs of young separated refugees.

Young people interviewed were often very thankful for being here, and although they have faced many difficult circumstances since arriving in England were determined to get a good education and make a positive contribution to society. We hope that this report is a step towards enabling young separated refugees to reach their full potential and achieve their ambitions.

Mike Aaranson
Director General
Save the Children

Contents

List of figures

Acknowledgements

This project has been supported by funding from The Diana, Princess of Wales Memorial Fund.

The author wishes to thank all the young people and professionals who we interviewed; Kieran Breen, who raised the funding and managed the project; Elli Free – who carried out some of the interviews and arranged many of the others – for co-ordinating the project; Perpetua Kirby of PK Research Consultancy, who helped to design the project and advised on the report; and all theSave the Children staff who contributed their expertise. Our thanks also to all the local authorities who co-operated with the research and who have responded to it.

The author also wishes to thank Terry Smith of the Refugee Council and Amy Weir of the Social Services Inspectorate of the Department of Health, for their valuable contribution.

This report draws on the seven local reports produced as part of the Young Separated Refugees Project. They were researched and written by Dr Edward Mynott and Dr Beth Humphries, Dr Andrew Dawson and Sarah Holding, Kathy Marriott, Clive Hedges and Andrew Render, and Kate Stanley.

About the author

Kate Stanley is a researcher with Save the Children. She co-designed the research for this report, conducted most of the interviews in London and the south-east and co-ordinated the research for this project in five other areas. She has worked as a researcher and project manager with vulnerable groups in Bosnia and Ghana and with an MP in Westminster.

1 Summary

Between July 2000 and February 2001, Save the Children carried out a study funded by The Diana, Princess of Wales Memorial Fund. Researchers spoke to 125 young asylum-seekers and refugees who have been separated from their parents or usual carers. They also spoke to 125 professionals working with these young people, to identify the constraints on and opportunities for the services provided to them. This study reveals what life is like for young separated refugees and makes a number of recommendations for action to improve their situation.

The policy context

By law, *unaccompanied* asylum-seeking and refugee children in England have the same legal entitlements as citizen children. This includes the right to education and healthcare and the rights enshrined in the Children Act (1989) and Human Rights Act (1998). Local authorities have responsibility for all unaccompanied children whom they define as "in need". Under the Children Act (1989) they have an obligation to provide a range and level of services appropriate to each child's needs.

Accompanied asylum-seeking children have lesser rights than citizen children, as they are supported through the National Asylum Support Service (NASS) and do not ordinarily have access to the provisions of the Children Act (1989) or access to child welfare benefits, although they do have the right to education and healthcare.

Save the Children believes that young separated refugees:
- should be entitled to all the rights enshrined in the UN Convention on the Rights of the Child 1989
- are children first and foremost
- are vulnerable and in need of care and protection
- are a potential asset to our society and not a burden.

The findings

- A significant number (26) of the young separated refugees we interviewed had chaotic and disturbing experiences on arrival and received little or no support. This pattern of experience continues in their contact with services, including education, health and social services.

- Many of the young separated refugees we interviewed had a substantial wait for their initial asylum decision and as a result experienced great anxiety and were unable to plan their future. There is little evidence that the Home Office commitment to speed up asylum decision times has had an impact on the claims of these young people. In addition, there is some evidence of inconsistent decision-making by the Home Office.

- The level of care and type of support received by young separated refugees depends more on which social services department they arrive at rather than on their individual needs.

- Young people aged 16 and 17 are particularly disadvantaged. Our research found that most young people arriving in England aged 16 or 17 are not "looked after" (that is, placed in public care) as a matter of policy and many are living in poor-quality or inappropriate accommodation, with little money or even vouchers issued by the local authority. Some placements where young people were living unsupervised with adults raised child protection concerns.

- Some social services departments enter into contracts with private companies, often located a considerable distance from their area, to provide care and accommodation. This arrangement is leaving these young people without adequate support, recourse to a social worker or independent complaints procedure.

- Education, particularly learning English, was a high priority for the young separated refugees we interviewed. However, access to opportunities and the level of support available vary from area to area. This adds to the sense of social exclusion felt by many young refugees. Many schools and colleges need more support to be able to cope with the needs of these young people. Bullying and harassment – both in and outside of education – had affected at least 30 percent of those interviewed.

- There is considerable confusion among young separated refugees about what will happen when they reach the age of 18. A number of professionals pointed to the potentially disastrous effects of the transition to adult services at 18, especially dispersal, which would entail the loss of friends and support.

- The vast majority of the young separated refugees we spoke to said they were physically healthy but many appeared to have emotional and possibly mental health problems, which were a result of their experiences at home and were compounded by their experiences here. Few had accessed mental health services.

Conclusion

The level of care and protection offered to these young people varied widely, depending on the experience, competence and willingness of local agencies to recognise and meet their needs.

Yet most demonstrated a determination to succeed and most were very grateful for the shelter and support offered to them – no matter how limited.

Despite their resilience and apparent maturity, young separated refugees deserve and require improvements in the standard of care and the protection they receive, whether they are under or over 16, unaccompanied or accompanied.

The findings highlight a number of gaps in the provision of services and detailed recommendations are made on action to improve the situation.

Summary of key recommendations

Central government

1. Government to remove its reservation on applying the UN Convention on the Rights of the Child 1989 to asylum-seeking and other non-citizen children.

2. Home Office to increase the grant to local authorities for the support of young separated refugees so that it meets the reasonable costs of support; and remove the distinction between the amount available to those under and those over the age of 16.

3. Home Office to improve procedures for assessing asylum applications from separated children in order to speed up decision times and ensure fair decisions.

4. Home Office and Department of Health to ensure that young separated refugees are supported in situ if they wish to be, and not dispersed, when they turn 18 years and are transferred to NASS.

5. Department of Health to specify appropriate forms of care for young separated refugees, including strengthening guidance on when Section 20 of the Children Act (1989) should be applied.

Local authorities

1. Social services to ensure that every young separated refugee receives a full needs-led assessment in line with the national framework for the assessment of children in need.

2. Social services to provide appropriate accommodation for young separated refugees by reducing reliance on unsupported hostel and bed-and-breakfast accommodation.

3. Social services to monitor all placements regularly, including "out of area" and private provider placements, in line with statutory obligations.

4. Social services to provide cash support to all young separated refugees supported under Section 17 of the Children Act (1989) and abolish the use of local authority vouchers for their support.

5. Establish inter-agency groups to ensure strategic planning of service provision to young separated refugees. This will include developing a database and improving information sharing within and between local authorities and external agencies.

6. Local education authorities and learning and skills councils to ensure that schools and colleges are equipped to provide appropriate English language courses, and schools and colleges to ensure that young separated refugees can get access to educational provision or learning.

7. Health authorities and primary care trusts to ensure that young separated refugees have access to mental health provision appropriate to their needs.

2   Introduction

The project

This study aims to give a voice to young people under the age of 18 who have come to England, separated from their parents or usual carers, to seek asylum. The study is part of a three-year project being undertaken by Save the Children and funded by The Diana, Princess of Wales Memorial Fund. Between July 2000 and February 2001, researchers talked to 125 young separated asylum-seekers and refugees across England (including London) about all aspects of their life since their arrival here.

A Young Person's Advisory Group made up of young separated refugees advised Save the Children on the project design, research process and publication of the reports.

We interviewed 125 professionals and other adults who work with young separated refugees, in order to understand what services are being provided to this group and the local constraints and opportunities for change.

Seven regional reports have been published (see bibliography for details) and this is the national report. Its aim is to reveal what life is like for young separated refugees in the care of a range of local authorities across England. It does not set out to compare their experiences with those of citizen children, although some disparities and similarities will be recognisable. The analysis highlights gaps in the provision of services, and recommendations are made on good practice in meeting the needs of these young people. Save the Children will use this report as the basis for campaigning for the development of good practice.

Since July 2001 Save the Children has begun to turn this information into action by implementing a series of pilot initiatives in the areas where research was carried out. These practical initiatives aim to start addressing the needs identified by the young people who participated in the study. They are run in partnership with voluntary and statutory organisations and young people themselves.

> *Save the Children believes that:*
> - Children and young people can and should participate in decisions about things that affect their lives, and they deserve to be listened to and taken seriously – Article 12, United Nations Convention on the Rights of the Child 1989 (UNCRC).
> - Asylum-seeking and refugee children are children first and foremost, and their immigration status is secondary to considerations of their best interests as children. As children, they are entitled to all the rights enshrined in the UNCRC, without discrimination.

Young asylum-seekers and refugees in the UK

There has been a significant overall increase in the number of young unaccompanied asylum-seekers arriving in the UK in recent years: from 631 in 1996 to 3,349 in 1999.[1] In 2000 the number of new asylum claims by unaccompanied minors fell to 2,735.[2] In 2000 the largest numbers of separated children came from the Federal Republic of Yugoslavia, Afghanistan, Somalia, Sri Lanka and Turkey (in descending order).[3]

The great majority of unaccompanied and accompanied children live in London and the south-east, particularly Kent. In the week ending 25 May 2001, there were 4,121 unaccompanied asylum-seeking children being supported by the London boroughs.[4]

There are no figures available for accompanied asylum-seeking children. Accompanied children are registered as being in the care of adults with whom they have some relationship. In 1999 asylum applications were received from 71,160 principal applicants with an estimated total of 20,070 dependants.[5]

There is currently no comprehensive database of separated children that includes both accompanied and unaccompanied children, whether seeking asylum or not. Nor does the Home Office produce separate figures on asylum decisions for separated young people.

This study involved only young people who had made a claim for asylum, and does not cover the experiences of those who have entered the UK under other immigration arrangements or illegally. Separated children who have entered the UK without coming to the attention of the immigration services may have been smuggled or trafficked. Some may be living in the community with friends, family or members of their community of origin. There is growing awareness of the exploitation of children by traffickers in prostitution, child pornography, sweatshop labour, forced begging and pickpocketing, or drug trafficking.[6] This is an area that requires urgent further research and, doubtless, criminal investigation.

The young people who participated in this study were not asked about how or why they came to England to seek asylum, as it is the intention of this report to look at only their experiences after their arrival here.

---

[1] Audit Commission, July 2000

[2] Home Office, Research and Development Statistics Directorate (RDSD), 25th September 2001

[3] Ibid

[4] London Asylum-Seekers Consortium, 25 May 2001

[5] Home Office, Asylum Liaison Unit, ISPD

[6] Ayotte and Williamson, 2001

3   The policy context

The United Nations Convention on the Rights of the Child 1989 (UNCRC)

In 1991 the UK Government signed and ratified the UNCRC. The United Nations High Commissioner for Refugees (UNHCR) has identified the following three Convention rights as key to ensuring the survival and development of refugee children.

> ### Article 2: Non-discrimination
> All rights apply to all children without exception, and the State has an obligation to protect children from any form of discrimination.

> ### Article 3: Best interests
> All actions concerning the child should take full account of his or her best interests.

> ### Article 12: The child's opinion
> The child has the right to express an opinion and have it taken into account, in any matter affecting

In addition, Article 22 grants special protection to asylum-seeking and refugee children.

> ### Article 22: Refugee children
> Special protection is to be granted to children who are refugees or seeking refugee status and the State is obliged to co-operate with organisations providing such protection and assistance.

The UK Government has reserved the right not to apply the UNCRC to asylum-seeking and other non-citizen children. However, it has asserted that the reservation does not inhibit its obligations to asylum-seeking and refugee children:

> *"The reservation does not inhibit the discharge of our obligations under Article 22. The UK is, of course, party to the 1951 Convention Relating to the Status of Refugees, and honours its obligations under this Convention in full."*

---

[7] Department of Health, 1994.

In a reply to a letter from a Member of Parliament, the then Home Office Minister, Barbara Roche MP, again asserted that the reservation does not interfere with the discharge of obligations under Article 22 of the UNCRC and justified the reservation on the following grounds:

> *"The reservation means that it is not possible for a child to seek entry to the United Kingdom or to seek to remain* **solely** [her emphasis]*in order to exercise his/her rights under the UN Convention on the Rights of the Child."* [8]

However, this is just one interpretation of the reservation and a future administration could choose to read it more widely.

Save the Children is campaigning for removal of the reservation on the grounds that all children in the UK should be explicitly guaranteed the same rights. The reservation clearly discriminates against asylum-seeking and refugee children.

The rights and entitlements of young separated refugees in England

This study shows that many asylum-seeking and refugee children do not receive the level of care and protection that they need. This is despite the fact that by law, *unaccompanied* asylum-seeking and refugee children in England have the same legal entitlements as citizen children. This includes the right to education and healthcare and the rights enshrined in the Children Act (1989) and Human Rights Act (1998).

Accompanied asylum-seeking children have lesser rights than citizen children. They are supported through the National Asylum Support Service (NASS); they do not ordinarily have access to financial support or accommodation through the Children Act (1989) or access to other child welfare benefits, although they do have the right to education and healthcare.

The European Union is currently developing directives on minimum standards in asylum procedures which include the treatment of separated children. It is hoped that the minimum standards will place pressure on the UK to improve its treatment of this group of young people.

---

[8] Barbara Roche MP, in letter to Win Griffiths MP, 4 January 2001.

The Children Act (1989)

It is very likely that all unaccompanied children meet the definition of children "in need" under Section 17 of the Children Act (1989) (see Figure 1, page 13), and should be registered with the social services department of the local authority where they first present themselves. They then become the responsibility of that local authority. In 1995 the Department of Health issued an excellent and comprehensive practice guide on the implementation of this legislation in relation to unaccompanied refugee children.[9]

Accompanied children who arrived in the UK before April 2000 would have been assessed, as part of a family, as being "in need" and would have had access to services through the local authority where they presented. Those who arrived after that date may have been assessed, as part of a family, by NASS, which accommodates and supports asylum-seeking families if they have been assessed as "destitute". If an unaccompanied child is reunited with family already residing in the UK, then they will join the support arrangements that are in place for the family.

If social services or the immigration service dispute that an applicant is aged under 18 years, then the burden of proof lies with the applicant and they will be referred to NASS.

Social services make an initial needs-led assessment to establish whether the applicant is a child and is "in need" as defined under Section 17 (see Figure 1). Once this is established the assessor will decide whether to provide services under Section 20 (see Figure 1). In practice, this stage is critical because it determines the level of care and support provided to the child.

Our research across England shows that unaccompanied children aged under 16 tend to be assessed as "in need" under Section 17 and receive services and accommodation under Section 20 (see 5.3, Accommodation). Although 16- and 17-year-olds are also assessed as "in need" under Section 17, they usually receive services and accommodation under Section 17 rather than under Section 20 (see Figure 6, page 34).

---

[9] Department of Health, 1995

Figure 1: Terms of the Children Act (1989)

> **"In Need":** A child is considered to be in need if *"he is unlikely to achieve or maintain or to have the opportunity of achieving and maintaining, a reasonable standard of health or development without the provision for him of services by a Local Authority"* (Section 17.10).
>
> **Section 17** gives local authorities a duty to *"safeguard and promote the welfare of children within their area who are in need… by providing a range and level of services appropriate to those children's needs"* (Section 17.1).
>
> **Section 20** states that children in need should be accommodated by the local authority in the following circumstances:
> 20.1 – *"Every Local Authority shall provide accommodation for any child in need who appears to them to require accommodation as a result of there being no person with parental responsibility for him; his being lost or abandoned; the person who has been caring for him being prevented (whether or not permanently, and for whatever reason) from providing him with suitable accommodation or care."*
> 20.3 – *"Every Local Authority shall provide accommodation for any child in need within their area who has reached the age of 16 and whose welfare the authority consider to be seriously prejudiced if they do not provide him with accommodation."*
> 20.4 – *"A Local Authority may provide accommodation for any child within their area (even though a person who has parental responsibility for him is able to provide him with accommodation) if they consider that to do so would safeguard or promote the child's welfare."*

In practice, assessments under Sections 17 and 20 have come to mean specific and differing packages of entitlements for young separated refugees. Accommodation provided under Section 20 usually means a foster care or residential home placement, but it may also include other arrangements as seem appropriate and have been approved by the Secretary of State. Accommodation provided under Section 17 may be anything from supported lodgings or a bed-and-breakfast to a privately rented shared house, as deemed appropriate by social services.

Assessment under Section 20 brings with it a wide range of services and support. Children will receive an allocated social worker, a care plan and cash financial support. Children supported under Section 20 are termed "looked after" and/or "accommodated", and are entitled to full leaving-care services.[10] Those assessed under Section 17 only will not necessarily receive any of these things, and may even receive vouchers issued by the local authority rather than cash financial support (see Figure 2, Page 15). In this report we employ the language used by

---

[10] Some restrictions may apply: for example, the Act is not retrospective – see the Children (Leaving Care) Act (2000).

local authorities to describe how they provide for young separated refugees and use the term "looked after" to refer to those who are accommodated under Section 20, and not those accommodated under Section 17.

Transition at 18 years

When a young person who has been in the care of social services reaches 18 years of age, a number of things may happen. NASS has stated that all unaccompanied children who applied for asylum after it assumed responsibility in the local authority where they applied,[11] should be referred to them for support on reaching the age of 18, which means they may be dispersed to another part of the country.

If their immigration status remains unresolved *and* they have been "looked after", they may be entitled to a package of support to help them make the adjustment from care to independent living under Section 24 of the Children Act (1989), which from October 2001 will be replaced by the Children (Leaving Care) Act (2000). Nonetheless, they will be also transferred to NASS for support. However, the Department of Health has issued welcome guidance on the Children (Leaving Care) Act (2000) in respect of young people in this position saying: "NASS will treat such 18-year old asylum-seekers sympathetically, and will not seek to disperse them, except in exceptional circumstances."

If their immigration status remains unresolved, *and* they have been supported through Section 17, they will be transferred to NASS.

However, in both cases if they applied for asylum before NASS took responsibility in the local authority where they applied, they will be transferred to leaving care services (if they have been "looked after") or the adult asylum team (if they have not been "looked after" and, sometimes, if they have).

If a young person has received a positive decision on their asylum claim, they will be entitled to full citizen benefits and be transferred to mainstream support services. If they have received a negative decision they will be transferred to NASS for the duration of their appeal, *or* if the appeal fails or they do not appeal, the Home Office will plan their enforced return to their country of origin.

---

[11] NASS assumed responsibility for the support of asylum-seeking adults and families in different areas of the country at different times during 2000. See Refugee Council Asylum Support briefing, March 2001.

Figure 2: The support of an unaccompanied child in England

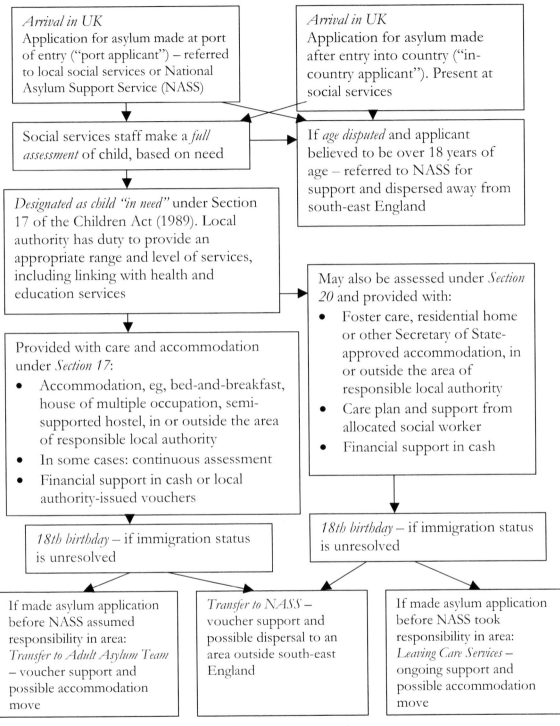

Arrival in UK
Application for asylum made at port of entry ("port applicant") – referred to local social services or National Asylum Support Service (NASS)

Arrival in UK
Application for asylum made after entry into country ("in-country applicant"). Present at social services

Social services staff make a *full assessment* of child, based on need

If *age disputed* and applicant believed to be over 18 years of age – referred to NASS for support and dispersed away from south-east England

Designated as child "in need" under Section 17 of the Children Act (1989). Local authority has duty to provide an appropriate range and level of services, including linking with health and education services

May also be assessed under *Section 20* and provided with:
- Foster care, residential home or other Secretary of State-approved accommodation, in or outside the area of responsible local authority
- Care plan and support from allocated social worker
- Financial support in cash

Provided with care and accommodation under *Section 17*:
- Accommodation, eg, bed-and-breakfast, house of multiple occupation, semi-supported hostel, in or outside the area of responsible local authority
- In some cases: continuous assessment
- Financial support in cash or local authority-issued vouchers

18th birthday – if immigration status is unresolved

18th birthday – if immigration status is unresolved

If made asylum application before NASS assumed responsibility in area: *Transfer to Adult Asylum Team* – voucher support and possible accommodation move

Transfer to NASS – voucher support and possible dispersal to an area outside south-east England

If made asylum application before NASS took responsibility in area: *Leaving Care Services* – ongoing support and possible accommodation move

OR if receive leave to remain

Refugee status – transfer to mainstream support services. Full entitlement to citizen benefits

Exceptional Leave to Remain (ELR) – transfer to mainstream support services. After four years with ELR, Indefinite Leave to Remain (ILR) likely to be granted and full entitlement to citizen benefits

OR if receive a refusal

Likely to begin *appeal process. Transfer to NASS during appeal. If lose appeal,* Home Office plans enforced return to country of origin. *If win appeal,* granted leave to remain and full entitlements as above.

Local authority funding

The responsibility for welfare policy on unaccompanied children lies with the Department of Health, but since 1999/2000 the Home Office has held the special grant that local authorities can claim for the support of unaccompanied children who are seeking asylum or have been awarded ELR or refugee status.

In 2000/2001, the grant structure changed so that those local authorities with responsibility for more than 100 unaccompanied children were able to claim up to £575 for each child aged under 16, and £300 for those over 16.[12] The range of eligible expenditure was also expanded in 2000/2001. It is worth noting that across England in 1999/2000, the average gross weekly expenditure per "looked after" child was £406 and in inner London the average was £575.[12]

In 2001 the grant was paid again retrospectively and local authorities did not know what the amounts would be until the last month of the financial year. While the increase and change to the grant structure is welcome, the retrospective nature of the grant limits local authorities' capacity for planning.

Possible changes to current arrangements

The Home Office has established a Working Party on Unaccompanied Asylum Seeking Children to look at a set of 17 proposals which would make significant changes to the arrangements described above. These proposals cover challenging age, casework decisions, care arrangements, enforcement and resources.

Of particular note are the proposals to:

- increase efforts to return unsuccessful applicants to their country of origin;

- set up a joint dispersal scheme for new unaccompanied children aged 16 and 17 presenting at social services departments in the south-east.

If these proposals were implemented, local authorities in south-east England might see a decrease in numbers of young separated refugees in the future.

On the other hand, authorities outside south-east England would be likely to see a further increase in the number of asylum-seeking children for whom they have responsibility. It would be imperative, therefore, that effective infrastructures and procedures were put in place in these authorities *before* dispersal took place, in order to ensure that the needs of these young people were met in full.

---

[12] Verbal communication, Association of London Government and Department of Health.

[13] Department of Health, *Social Services Performance in 1999-2000*, published at www.doh.gov.uk.

It is hoped that this report will contribute to the discussions surrounding these proposals, so that the best interests of young separated refugees will be taken into account. In addition, we hope that the Government will take particular care to learn the lessons from the existing dispersal system, which has been fraught with problems and not delivered according to the original principles.

Important legislation and initiatives relating to young separated refugees

Education rights and personal education plans

The Education Act (1944) describes local authorities' duty to assume the parent's responsibility to provide the child in need with "efficient full-time education suitable to his age, ability and aptitude". Local education authorities have a duty to ensure that education is available for all children of compulsory school age in their area, appropriate to their age, abilities and aptitudes and any special education needs they may have. This duty applies irrespective of a child's immigration status.[13]

There is a statutory obligation to provide full-time education to children aged under 16; however, both the Human Rights Act (Protocol 1, Article 2, 1998) and the UNCRC (Article 28) assert the right of everyone to education.

Further education colleges are not under a duty to accept asylum-seekers on to their courses but may choose to do so. If a college accepts an asylum-seeker on a course it can apply at that point to the learning and skills council for funding.

Personal education plans (PEPs) were designed by the Department for Education and Employment (now the Department for Education and Skills – DfES) to assist local authorities to meet their obligations to "looked after" children. It is a tool for those working with "looked after" children, to enable them to create strategic plans to meet children's educational needs, and address the poor outcomes for this group.

Human Rights Act (1998)

Public authorities have a duty not to act incompatibly with the rights set out in the Human Rights Act (1998) and in some cases they have a positive obligation to act compatibly with the Act. Young separated refugees are entitled to enjoy all

---

[14] National Asylum Support Service, Draft Education - Policy Bulletin 63, 30 August 2001.

the rights in the Act without discrimination. The rights enshrined in the Act can be summarised as follows:

Article 2: The right to life
Article 3: Freedom from torture, inhuman and degrading treatment
Article 4: Freedom from slavery or servitude, forced or compulsory labour
Article 5: The right not to be unlawfully detained
Article 6: The right to a fair hearing
Article 8: The right to respect for private and family life, for home and correspondence
Article 9: Freedom of religion, thought and conscience
Article 10: Freedom of expression and freedom to receive information without interference
Article 11: Freedom of association
Article 14: The right not to be discriminated against in the enjoyment of these rights
Protocol 1, Article 2: No person shall be denied the right to education.

Immigration and Asylum Act (1999)

The Immigration and Asylum Act (1999) formally established a system of dispersal of asylum-seekers across England. The aim was to spread the "burden of responsibility" for asylum-seekers across the country and away from London and south-east England. The Act set up the National Asylum Support Service (NASS) to provide accommodation and financial support to asylum-seekers.

Although the Act does not apply to unaccompanied children, and they remain the responsibility of local authorities, it does have important implications for them. Not least of these is the further disruption dispersal will cause separated asylum-seekers turning 18 years.

The Act proscribes the use of child welfare legislation for the financial support of accompanied children; instead, the principal applicant receives accommodation and vouchers, supplemented by £10 cash each week. This means that accompanied children must live with the stigma and limitations of vouchers.

Quality Protects

Quality Protects is a major three-year programme, launched by the Department of Health in 1998, designed to improve the management and delivery of social services to children. It focuses on children who are "looked after", in the child protection system, or disabled. If the local authority meets specific targets in relation to these children, ring-fenced money is released to further improve services. Local authorities are required to submit a Quality Protects Management Action Plan (MAP) each year to the Department of Health.

Young separated refugees can be included in Quality Protects targets if they have been "looked after", but not all local authorities have taken the opportunity to specifically name them in their MAP; generally, those young people assessed under Section 17 only are not included. One former social services manager has described the potential of Quality Protects to help meet their needs:

"Though we are a long way, as a society, from seeing young asylum-seekers as children first and foremost, Quality Protects may be the best chance, in the foreseeable future, to identify and plan to meet their needs."[14]

National Assessment Framework (2000)

The statutory guidance contained in the *Framework for the assessment of children in need and their families*, published in 2000 by the Department of Health, Department for Education and Employment and the Home Office, provides professionals with a tool for making evidence-based assessments of a child's situation and needs. The framework notes that young separated refugees "will require particular care and attention during assessment".

Connexions

Connexions is a new service to provide information, guidance and advice for 13- to 19-year-olds to help them make the most of their educational, vocational and developmental opportunities, in order to prepare them for a successful transition to work and adult responsibilities.[15] Connexions will give priority to young people who are at greatest risk of not making a successful transition to adulthood, including young people in public care.

Full and Equal Citizens (2001)

Full and Equal Citizens is a Home Office strategy for the integration of those with leave to remain, published in 2001. Among other things, the strategy aims to include refugees as equal members of society and to help to develop their potential and contribution to the cultural and economic life of the country. The pledges in the action plan that have particular relevance to children are: NASS, the DfES and the Local Government Association will collate good practice on refugee education and disseminate it widely. The DfES will continue discussions with refugee organisations to consider gaps in English as a Second or Other Language (ESOL) provision. The DfES will consider setting minimum standards for ESOL, and a possible pilot initiative followed by pilot orientation courses in 2001/2002.

---

[15] Little, 2001.

[16] NCVCCO, 2001.

Recent research about young separated refugees

A great deal has been written about refugees and refugee children (see Audit Commission, 2000; Candappa and Egharevba, 2000; Rutter and Jones, 1998 on the UK). However, little has been written about young separated refugees in the UK and less still based on consultation with young people themselves, although the following reports all point to a need for it.

The Separated Children in Europe Programme (SCEP) is a joint initiative of four European members of the Save the Children Alliance and the United Nations High Commissioner for Refugees (UNHCR). The SCEP published a *Statement of Good Practice*[16] which sets out 11 first principles which are the basis for good practice from the point of arrival to the development of a durable solution which is in the best interests of the child.

Save the Children UK and the Refugee Council recently reported[17] on the performance of the UK in relation to the principles laid out in the *Statement of Good Practice*. The UK was found to be seriously lacking in a number of key areas: care of separated children, trafficking for exploitation, asylum procedure, detention of separated children, age assessment, family tracing, contact and reunification, and guardianship for separated children. In some areas the UK was identified as demonstrating good or better than average practice: for example, the Children Act (1989) provisions on culturally appropriate care, the existence of specially trained staff assessing children's applications, and the system of the independent Panel of Advisers.

Supporting unaccompanied children in the asylum process[18] provides a comprehensive study of the asylum process and, in particular, the role of legal representatives in supporting unaccompanied children, based on interviews with young people and professionals. For this reason the present report does not focus on the role of legal representatives and the Home Office, and legal professionals were not interviewed. Nevertheless, it does of course discuss the issues that were raised by young people in relation to their asylum claim.

A survey of local authorities by Barnado's[19] reached similar conclusions to those of a report by the influential Audit Commission:[20]

---

[17] UNHCR/Save the Children, 2000 (2nd ed).

[18] Ayotte and Williamson, 2001.

[19] Ayotte, 1998.

[20] Stone, 2000.

[21] Audit Commission, 2000.

"Whilst the legislation is clear it is apparent that it is applied inconsistently resulting in varied and inconsistent service provision."

Local authorities blamed inconsistent service on a lack of guidance from central government, a shortfall in resources and a shortage of appropriate accommodation. Barnado's called on the Government to address the resource issue, and local authorities to undertake full needs assessments.

Children of the Storm's report, *Other People's Children*,[21] focused on the views of professionals in three local authorities and concluded that there is an urgent need for central government leadership and guidelines on the treatment of unaccompanied children.

The present report contributes to this body of knowledge by providing evidence of the experiences of 125 young refugees, often through their own words. It is designed to promote improvements in local service provision as well as contributing to local and national policy debates.

---

[22] Munoz, 2000.

4   Methodology

Selection of areas

The study was carried out in Greater Manchester, Oxford, the West Midlands, London, Newcastle, and Yorkshire and Humberside. The local authorities which participated in this research were selected partly on the basis of the locations of Save the Children regional offices, but also because they represented a good range of areas, including some with high numbers of young separated refugees and others with very small numbers of young separated refugees or, indeed, of ethnic minorities, some with ports within their boundaries and dispersal areas. This report pulls out the national themes and variations across the areas and considers the broader implications of local situations.

The young people

Interviews were held with 125 young people, who were contacted through a range of statutory and voluntary organisations. Flyers were produced and distributed in 13 languages, explaining the project and inviting participation. A Young Person's Advisory Group of young separated refugees was set up to advise on the research and initiatives.

Interpreters were used whenever requested by the young person. On occasions, the interpreters were young separated refugees themselves, and formed part of the interview group.

All young people who participated in the research were fully informed about the aims of the research and the limit placed on the confidentiality of their statements: that is, the interviews were anonymous and confidential to the extent that the only circumstances in which information about a named young person might be passed on to another person would be if the young person discloses a serious risk of harm to them while they have been in the UK.

Sixty-five young people were interviewed alone, and 64 were interviewed in groups by the authors of the local and national reports. A number of the young people were interviewed more than once. Most of the interviews were based around a semi-structured interview schedule derived from issues highlighted by previous interviews and research findings. The schedule covered the topics of accommodation, adult support, education, social activities, immigration issues and health. The remaining interviews took the form of informal conversations.

Information about support services, rights and entitlements was taken to the interviews and referrals were made to support services where appropriate and where requested.

The research took a reflexive approach in which consideration was given to the impact of the researchers and to barriers to the young people's participation, and attempts made to overcome these where possible.

The adults

One-to-one interviews were carried out with 125 professionals and other adults working with young separated refugees. These interviews provided a good framework for understanding the local political, financial and social constraints. In turn, this assisted with the formulation of practical recommendations.

The sample

This is a qualitative report and the sample is not statistically representative of all young separated refugees or professionals who work with them in England. However, the research does provide a good overview of the sorts of views, experiences and needs of these young people and the views of those who work with them.

Figure 3: Table to show profile of young people interviewed

Country of origin	No.	Age	No.
Afghanistan	24	Under 16	12
Albania	9	16-17	84
Angola	4	18-20	29
Congo	1		
Croatia	1	**Gender**	
Eritrea	4	Male	105
Ethiopia	5	Female	20
Iran	2		
Iraq	6	**Immigration status**	
Kosovo	47	Refugee	7
Kurdistan/Kurdish	3	Exceptional Leave to Remain	7
Macedonia	1	Asylum-seeker	81
Montenegro	3	Refused	5
Romania	1	Unknown	25
Rwanda	1		
Somalia	6		
South America	1	**Family situation**	
Zaire	1	Accompanied	26
Zimbabwe	4	Unaccompanied	92
Uganda	1	Unknown	7

Figure 4: Table to show the profile of professionals interviewed

Sector	No.
Education	32
Social services	38
Health	13
Youth services	11
Voluntary sector	17
Private sector	3
Other	11
Total	**125**

Limitations

The pace of change in some areas is fast, and some of the activities and practices described in this study may have changed or even finished since the research took place. We have presented the key themes raised by young separated refugees in the areas studied at the end of 2000 and the beginning of 2001 and we believe they are applicable across England.

5 The findings

In this chapter the experiences of young separated refugees are examined in relation to the services provided for their care and protection in several regions of England. Common themes across geographical areas are identified and regional differences highlighted.

The longer case studies presented illustrate more clearly the complexity of the lives of these young people and the interdependence of various aspects of their lives. They also show some of the many ways in which young people themselves shape their own lives.

The key issues of concern for the young people are explored in turn. These are: arrival and age determination (p. 25), assessment (p. 33), accommodation (p. 40), support from social workers (p. 55), financial support (p. 64), transition at 18 years (p.68), education (p. 71), social networks (p. 87), immigration issues (p. 101) and health (p. 109).

5.1 Arrival and age determination

"I went to the police and the police didn't help me because I was out of the airport and I was supposed to inform the police before I came out." (Boy, aged 15 on arrival)

Main findings

- At least one quarter of the young people we spoke to had chaotic experiences on arrival and received little or no support.

- Young people usually present to a particular social services department as a result of chance rather than design, although a minority do make decisions to present in a certain place, often because they have friends or family in the area.

- Some local authorities are concerned that if they improve their provision they will attract young separated refugees to their area.

- Only one social services department had its own written age-determination guidelines, and in many places practices are rudimentary.

5.1.1 Port applicants

Young separated refugees may present themselves to or be identified by immigration officials at the port of entry ("port applicants"). Immigration officers will then refer them to the local social services department or a voluntary agency for onward referral to the National Asylum Support Service (NASS), depending on how old they believe them to be.

The Refugee Council's Panel of Advisers request details of all unaccompanied asylum-seeking children who are identified at a port of entry in order to provide short-term support and advice about the asylum process and welfare issues. Their success in making contact with the children will depend on the accuracy of the details taken down by immigration officers. Our research suggests that in some cases these can be inaccurate (see box below).

> In the case of one 15-year-old boy, immigration officials were unable to find an interpreter who spoke his language so they found one who spoke another dialect of the same language group. The boy later realised that the interpreter had mistaken his first name for his surname. Similarly, another boy had his date of birth recorded as 1979 instead of 1983 because the interpreter did not understand him properly. Mistakes like this are very difficult to change later and can even undermine the apparent validity of supporting evidence on an asylum application.

5.1.2 In-country applicants

PRESENTING AT SOCIAL SERVICES

Those who are not identified at the port of entry by immigration officers must present themselves for support at a social services department ("in-country applicants"). One young person described how difficult this can be without appropriate support from public services.

One boy arrived at an airport with an agent who disappeared on arrival. The boy waited at the airport all night for the agent to return. Eventually he went outside the airport, and saw a police car. He asked the police for help but they told him they could not help him and he should go back inside the airport. He waited another day in the airport. Then again he asked the police outside for help, and this time he got a different response:

> "The police told me they gonna give me a hotel or something and I sat in the car and I came to… like a busy market thing. The police drop me there and he said to me, 'Here's [the city], very nice place, tourist city, you can go and enjoy yourself there.' I said to them, 'I need some place to rest' – I was very tired. They said I had to go and left [me] there."

The 15-year-old, who spoke very little English, had £120, and he spent the next five days in the cold sleeping rough in a park. Eventually a stranger told him to go to the local authority offices and after two more nights in the cold he made it there. After waiting in reception for some time a member of staff interviewed him and said they could not help because there were no hotels available and he had to go back to the airport. But the boy refused to move, as he had no money left. After two hours, another man appeared and this one was more helpful:

> "This man was treating me very good and he took me to a hotel that night. I couldn't sleep thinking I was dreaming or something."

Nearly all the other young people we spoke to who had been in contact with the police described them as "friendly" or something equally positive. The Association of Chief Police Officers has recently produced the ACPO Guide to Meeting the Policing Needs of Asylum-Seekers and Refugees[23] which asserts that "asylum-seekers and refugees are entitled to the same protection to live free from crime, harassment and intimidation as any other members of our society". However, a second boy's experience of the police was less than helpful.

---

[23] Association of Chief Police Officers, 2001.

This boy presented himself to the police when he got off a lorry that had brought him into the country. Fellow travellers told him to say he was 20 years old rather than give his real age of 16. Despite the fact there was clearly some doubt about his age, the police took him at his word and put him in a cell with adult asylum-seekers.

Some time later the police took him to an airport deportation centre where he was held for five days. He said the centre was like *"a cell. It was something like a house inside, without windows, without nothing. It was a room in a block. It was many people there."*

After finally gaining access to a solicitor over the phone, he was taken to a detention centre where he was held for a further seven days before he was interviewed, acknowledged as a minor and released into the care of social services – after a total of 13 days.

Many young people (at least 26) had similarly chaotic and disturbing experiences on arrival. Their stories show how a combination of chance and advice from random contacts can often determine where they eventually present for support.

One boy caught a train to London, which he knew was a big city where he would be able to lodge an asylum application. He got on the Hammersmith and City underground line, imagining it would take him to "the city", and got off at the last stop where he presented to social services.

Others, of course, make more deliberate choices in the hope of securing a better quality of life, like the girl in the example below who was pregnant and particularly in need of decent accommodation and support.

One pregnant 16-year-old presented in London and was placed in a hostel with young men, where she felt intimidated. The hostel was in a very poor state of repair. She was receiving local authority issued vouchers instead of cash, and could not use these to get around on public transport. When she complained to social services about the conditions she felt they were not interested and had no intention of helping her.

A contact from her country of origin was living in another city in the south-east and experiencing much better conditions so she decided to leave London and presented herself there. Due in part to her pregnancy, the social services department in the new city accepted her into its care.

Another young person spent a few weeks at a southern town and a week in London before moving further north. Conditions in both London and the town seem to have been such that this young person thought it would be an advantage to be in an area where there were fewer asylum-seekers:

> *"I was in* [town] *and it wasn't very good, there were a lot of… asylum-seekers, and they used to fight with English a lot. I just thought it would be better for me to move. I… thought, if you go north there won't be a lot of asylum-seekers and that, so you can get some help. You can get support."*

A number of local authorities admitted to researchers that they were apprehensive about improving the quality of service they provided to young separated refugees in case they got a reputation and attracted an increased share of new applicants. One social worker described his frustration with the reluctance of senior management to tackle the issue for this reason:

> *"I think the main block is around anxiety in senior management. It's like 'if we give the remit and work in a particular way with these ten young people, we then set a precedent… the floodgates will open'. It's almost like 'don't meet their needs because if you do, loads more will come'."*

The examples showing how young people are guided by chance represent the majority in our research. Those few young people we spoke to who did make deliberate and considered decisions to go to a particular place did so on the basis of either the presence of relatives or friends in an area or because they felt forced out of an area by poor conditions. If all local authorities improved the standard of care they provided, young people would not be subjected to conditions that force them to move.

THE PANEL OF ADVISERS

Those who present directly to social services are also eligible for support from the Panel of Advisers but whether or not they receive this support depends partly on social workers knowing about the Panel and forwarding the young person's details to them. Our research found that social services staff in eight local authorities had not even heard of the Panel. In the following example, the police had clearly heard of the Panel but failed to ensure the young people were referred to them or even to social services.

> One young boy described how he and his friend had been identified by police after getting off a lorry near a city in the Midlands. They were taken to the police station where they were told someone from the Refugee Council would collect them, but in the end they were released to wander the streets and resorted to asking passers-by what to do. Eventually they got advice in a shop:
>
> *"We told the Pakistani shopkeepers that we were going to London, but they advised us, because… London was far away from this place: 'You had better go to Birmingham.' So we didn't go to London and we came to this city."*
>
> They arrived in the city but as they did not know anyone there: *"We were wandering and we spent two nights and we didn't have any place."* Finally they met a fellow countryman who took them to his home and on to the Refugee Council the next day.

Receiving support from a Panel Adviser will also depend on the availability of an adviser in a particular area and at that time. The Home Office funds the Panel to provide a crucial service but the funding is insufficient to ensure that Advisers are able to see all young separated refugees arriving in England. Those they do see they must seek to limit the number of hours spent supporting them.

5.1.3 Age determination

Once a young person has been identified as a separated refugee their age will be assessed. This is frequently a rudimentary exercise.

Only one of the social services departments we looked at had produced its own written guidelines on age-determination procedures (although another was developing them) and only one had any guidelines at all on working with separated refugees (although two were developing them). These guidelines gave the social workers a tool to assist their decision-making.

Age determination begins with an immediate assessment made by an immigration officer or social worker, taking into account the views of other professionals, the information the young person provides and their appearance. If after due consideration, the applicant is believed to be over 18 they will be referred to NASS for support. If not, they will be referred to social services. The burden of proof lies with the young person; if they are able to verify their age at a later date, NASS is required to refer them back to the social services department where they first presented for care.

None of young people we spoke to reported having had their age disputed. However, in one of the local authorities we looked at, policies had been adopted on the presumption that significant numbers presenting to them were actually adults claiming to be children. The problem of how to satisfactorily deal with cases where an applicant's age was in dispute was resolved by treating all those who said they were 16 years or over in the same way as single adults.

According to a social work professional in this authority, the provision for 16- and 17-year-olds is similar to that usually received under Section 17 of the Children Act (1989), but because the money comes through a separate grant they are not really assessed under the Act. The assessment form used for 16- and 17-year-olds is the same as for single adults, and while the social worker completing it "may be aware there are different needs because they are under 18… the form is focused around adult needs". A second social services employee confirmed that the current system for 16- and 17-year-olds would never operate in respect of citizen children, saying simply: "It is completely discriminatory."

This arrangement may resolve the issue of determining age from an administrative point of view, and ensures that adults are not mistakenly placed in a child's system; but it does not ensure that children are not placed in an adult's system. Nor does it resolve the fundamental fact that age must be fully assessed in order to provide the additional support and protection to which separated children are entitled under the Children Act (1989). It is clear that, in this case, the status of the young people as asylum-seekers is given precedence over their status as children. In a number of areas uncertainty over the age of many applicants was blamed for the unwillingness of certain social services teams to support asylum teams or of social services, more generally, to provide an appropriate level of care to young separated refugees.

X-rays are not standard immigration procedure (although they are carried out in specific cases, for example, where immigrants are suspected of carrying drugs) but three young people we spoke to reported having been X-rayed and told that this was part of standard procedures. All three were 17 years old and African. One of them said:

> "*Some* [immigration] *officers are very rough and when you tell them your story of what has happened to you, they say things like 'nonsense'.*"

X-rays have been suggested as a way of helping determine age but the Royal College of Paediatricians[24] has unequivocally stated that X-rays should not be used to determine age, not least because they are inaccurate as well as potentially harmful. Instead they advocate "a holistic examination of the child".

The Refugee Council's adviser on unaccompanied minors supports a holistic approach:

> *"Age assessment, like any assessment, is a process not a single event. Only through direct work with a child and an holistic assessment of their experiences, skills and needs, can we begin to make a judgement of which age range a child or young person is likely to fit in to."* [25]

She adds that young people can often appear older than they claim to be on arrival as the experience of exile has an impact on a young person. In our research a number of social work practitioners agreed that the only way to really assess age is to observe and interact with a young person over a period of time.

---

[24] Royal College of Paediatricians and Child Health, 1999.

[25] Personal communication, 10 July 2001.

5.2 Assessment – the crucial step

"We are facing breaking point in achieving appropriate family placements for these young people... [And] we are in severe difficulty in providing appropriate support to unaccompanied minors." (Senior social services manager, in correspondence)

Main findings

- We did not identify a single case where an adult carer accompanying a separated child had been assessed for their suitability to take responsibility for the child.

- The grant structure for the support of young separated refugees and existing local government strategies act as disincentives to placing young separated refugees aged 16 or 17 in the "looked after" system.

- The outcome of an assessment is frequently predetermined by whether a child is accompanied or unaccompanied, under or over 16 years and what resources are available to support them. It seems that assessments are being compromised in order to make them fit practical circumstances, such as the availability and cost of placements.

The quality of care received by young separated refugees from social services departments in England is determined by a handful of closely related factors. These are set out in the diagram below.

Figure 5: The factors affecting the care received by a child and the links between these factors

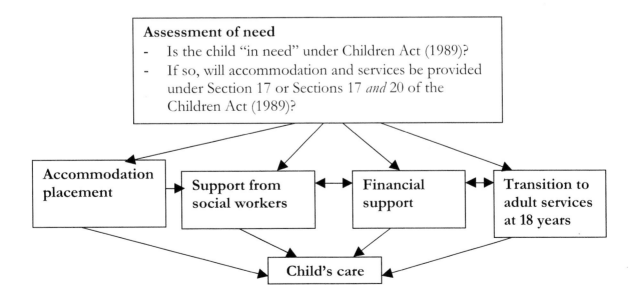

All children who may be "in need" are entitled to a full assessment of their needs. The assessment will determine whether they are "in need" and, if so, what level of services they require; that is, do they need to be "looked after" under Section 20 or provided with services under Section 17 alone? If they are "looked after" under Section 20 they will receive accommodation (usually foster care or a residential home), a care plan, an allocated social worker and cash financial support. If they are under Section 17 their accommodation will usually be private rented independent accommodation, they will receive financial support in either cash or vouchers and are less likely to have a care plan or allocated social worker (see Figure 6). It is at the discretion of the social services department whether or not to provide financial support in cash or issue their own vouchers (it is not government policy to issue separated children with vouchers, as it is in the case of single adults and families). The assessment is therefore crucial in determining a child's experiences. The key factors affecting the outcome of this assessment in practice are illustrated in Figure 6 below.

Figure 6: Diagram to show how practice and services provided to young separated refugees vary according to whether unaccompanied or accompanied and age

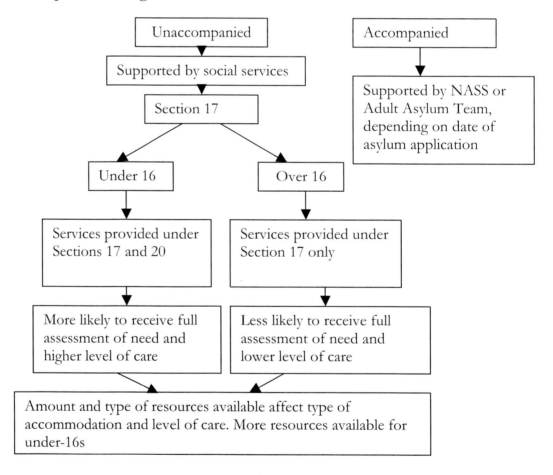

5.2.1 Unaccompanied or accompanied

The assessment begins with ascertaining whether a child is accompanied or unaccompanied. This will affect how they are supported. It is very likely that all unaccompanied minors (ie, under 18 years) meet the definition of a child "in need" (see Figure 1) and should be cared for under the provisions of the Children Act (1989). However, young refugees who are accompanied by an adult carer or who have relatives already living in the country will be treated under family arrangements through the National Asylum Support Service (NASS) (or through an adult asylum team – under interim arrangements or mainstream benefits – if they applied for asylum before NASS took over responsibility for asylum-seekers in the area they applied; or they may be supporting themselves through employment).

We did not identify a single case where the adult carer or relative in this arrangement was assessed for their suitability to take responsibility for the child. Social workers cited cases where a child had been handed over to the care of a relative and the relative received an increase in their Income Support to provide for them. In this case, the child is discharged from the care of the local authority and the family is not supported by social services. There is no assessment of the relative/s, which raises child protection concerns for the child. One senior social services manager admitted.

"The management of risk in relation to those young people who are placed with 'family' members, often with quite tenuous links, is… of major concern."

However, it is possible to safeguard the welfare of children who are placed with adults who are not their usual carers through a variety of measures. For example, Regulation 11 of the Children Act (1989) may be used as a way of assessing the suitability of an adult to care for a specific known child. It is a less broad-ranging process than the usual assessment for foster carers but all the questions are relevant. Under Regulation 11, responsibility for the child would ordinarily stay with the team that works with unaccompanied minors, and the fostering team would pay the carer but not support them.

Case study: Albert

Albert's story demonstrates the vulnerability of children who are accompanied but nonetheless separated from their usual carer. This vulnerability is particularly acute when the carers are not fully assessed for their suitability. Albert's story also shows how placement outside of the local authority with responsibility can create a vacuum of care. His situation is compounded by, and in turn exacerbates, his health problems.

Albert arrived at a port in late 2000, when he was 16 years old. Translating Albert's own words, his interpreter described his arrival in the UK:

> *"He had a fit in the lorry* [Albert has chronic asthma] *so* [he was] *taken to hospital by immigration. After a few minutes he was discharged… He was taken to the police station, but he could not concentrate after the fit. The interpreter* [who spoke a different dialect of his language and was from a different country] *was not very friendly and made him have* [a] *recorded interview. The man was arguing with him rather than asking questions."*

Albert has siblings who have been living here for some time. Soon after his arrival he was moved to live in a house in the north-west with his brother and his brother's family, but he wanted to live with his sister in London. Responsibility for Albert's welfare lies with either his brother in the north-west or the London borough where his sister lives – this was unclear and compounded the problems he faced.

Things worked out badly in the house with his brother and Albert left:

> *"His brother was in custody and his brother was beaten by* [supporters of a political group in his country of origin] *and he is not very well mentally and he gets very angry very easily… and they have a big problem for a small word. So he* [Albert] *leaves before it gets worse – it's better to get out."*

Even though he has left the house, his brother still receives the money for Albert's care from social services. According to Albert this totals £114 per week for six people and "it was not even enough for food".[26] So Albert has no money at all – he walks an hour each way to school.

Nor does he have anywhere to live. He cannot tell a social worker what has happened because he has never met one and he does not even know how to contact social services. He has spent the last couple of nights living with another asylum-seeking boy and his father. There is no bed for him there and the boy and his father only have £47 a week to live on. The interpreter said he did not want to stay there: *"He feels he is not ready to go back to the Albanian people because the money they get is not enough for them to survive themselves, so how can they support him as well?"* He has been doing their laundry in payment for his stay with them. He does not know where he will stay tonight.

The stress of his daily life is making his asthma worse and *"he is getting worried, and the problem he has will put him in very big trouble"*. He has been to the doctor several times but the doctor continues to prescribe the medication he had in his country of origin and says it will take a year to get an appointment to see a specialist.

His poor health has affected his attendance at school and he feels *"he is wasting his time sitting in classes in English. He wants more English tuition. He gets five to six hours a week."*

---

[26] It is worth noting that the actual entitlement of this family should have been £181.97 a week under NASS.

5.2.2 Under or over 16 years

"What you get depends on what social services department you are with, things are definitely getting more difficult as I get older." (Boy, aged 18)

Social services are obliged to provide any unaccompanied child with a range and level of services appropriate to their needs. Practice has developed such that many local authorities automatically provide accommodation and services to 16- and 17-year-olds under Section 17 and to under 16-year-olds under Section 20. Eighty-two per cent (80 out of 97) of 16- and 17-year-olds were receiving support through Section 17 (and most of the remaining 18 per cent arrived aged under 16).

One local authority we looked at has written guidelines that make clear that the particular needs of each child should take priority in assessing the kind of support offered to them. It also states, however, that only in "exceptional circumstances" would a 16- or 17-year-old be "looked after" under Section 20. A social worker in this local authority reported that in reality, providing care under Section 20 for a newly arrived 16- or 17-year-old "just wouldn't happen".

It is common for social services departments to take the approach that 16- and 17-year-olds do not need to be "looked after". In fact, in some areas there is little recognition of their duties to 16- and 17-year-olds, as this social worker indicated:

> *"The* [social services] *department has not got an active policy in place for 16- and 17-year-olds; there is no long-term policy of commitment."*

This practice of service division based on age makes exact age determination very important as it will determine the level of care and support provided. It assumes age is the prime determinant of need, but this approach is not well grounded in the legislation, as all unaccompanied children aged under 18 are entitled to be accommodated under Section 20 by virtue of the fact that they are not accompanied by a carer.

5.2.3 Full needs assessment

"It's easier to meet what we perceive to be their needs rather than asking them or taking their previous life experience into account." (Social worker)

The Department of Health's practice guide on unaccompanied asylum-seeking children[27] states that assessments should be carried out as shown on the next page.

---

[27] Social Services Inspectorate, 1995.

> **Good practice**
> All case assessment, review and planning processes, will necessarily include *at least* the following:
> 1. Personal and family history
> 2. Exile history and its effects
> 3. Contact with family, friends and community
> 4. Legal and immigration status
> 5. Education/employment history and plans
> 6. Health – physical and emotional
> 7. Language, religion and diet
> 8. Placement plans
> 9. Physical resources (ie, clothes etc)
> 10. Leaving-care plans, where appropriate
> 11. Support for carers.

A number of professionals believed that the development of a thorough approach to needs assessment and a flexible package of support was especially important for this group because their needs are different from those of their peers who have always lived in this country. As numerous social workers pointed out, they may be mature in many ways but they need help with English language and everyday tasks, such as shopping.

> **Good practice**
> In some authorities care is taken to match individual needs with placement. For example, two of the local authorities had taken steps to explicitly apply the new statutory *Framework for the assessment of children in need and their families* (Department of Health et al, 2001) to the assessment of the needs of young separated refugees. This will ensure that every young person registering with social services will be assessed across a range of welfare issues, and health and education services will be informed of their particular needs within one week of them registering. Of course, this should happen in all cases as a matter of policy but it is highlighted here as good practice because it does not.

5.2.4 Resources

Social workers aim to recommend care for a child that it is possible to deliver. Care will be planned with resource constraints in mind. These constraints may include the Quality Protects Management Action Plan aim of reducing the number of children in general who are "looked after", which may not be compatible with the need to accommodate young separated refugees in a manner appropriate to their needs. Secondly, there is a shortage of foster carers in many parts of the country. Finally, it is clearly more expensive to place a child in foster care or a residential home than in independent accommodation.

These constraints combine to put pressure on local authorities not to place young separated refugees in the "looked after" system. A further disincentive to placing those aged 16 or 17 in the "looked after" system is the structure of the central government grant for the support of young separated refugees, which is worth less for those aged 16 or 17 than for those aged under 16. One social work professional confirmed that in their area placement policy follows the government grant structure:

> "We receive more funding from the Home Office for those under 16 than for the older ones... It seems like the over-16-year-olds are automatically accommodated under Section 17 as we get less financial support for them."

A number of local authorities, particularly those in London and the south-east, where accommodation costs tend to be higher, felt that the grant was too small to cover all the costs associated with the care of young separated refugees. It should also be noted that the use of Section 20 to support a young person triggers the local authority's responsibility to provide leaving care services which, of course, have resource implications.

The number of inappropriate placements we identified (see section 5.3) strongly indicates that if full needs-led assessments are taking place, they are not being implemented consistently. In fact, it would seem that assessments are being compromised in order to fit the practical circumstances, such as the availability and cost of placements.

5.3 Accommodation

Main findings

- Those who are placed in a hostel, bed and breakfast or private rented accommodation receive a considerably lower standard of care than those who are placed in foster care or residential home accommodation.

- Those who are placed at a significant distance from the local authority that has responsibility for them receive a lower standard of care than they would if they were resident in the local authority with responsibility.

- There is a shortage of appropriate foster carers in many parts of the country which reduces social services placement options.

- In some areas, many young separated refugees were living with adults in unsupervised accommodation and this raises child protection concerns.

- None of the local authorities we looked at ran an independent visitors scheme to which young separated refugees had access.

- It is common for young people to be placed in locations where there is no knowledge or appreciation of their culture, food or language.

- Young people felt private accommodation providers were unresponsive to complaints about conditions in their housing. Social services were failing to adequately monitor these placements.

Key factors affecting accommodation placement of a young person:

- Is the child "looked after"? Then they are likely to be accommodated in foster or residential care.
- Is the child not "looked after"? Then they are likely to be accommodated in a hostel, bed and breakfast or private rented accommodation.
- Is the child not "looked after" and there is a shortage of placements in the vicinity of the local authority with responsibility for them? Then they are likely to be placed in accommodation in the care of a private agency out of the area of the authority with responsibility for them.

5.3.1 Foster care

"Foster care has been very important, it has helped me a lot. Every Monday I saw my social worker – really good support."

The first choice of many social services departments is to place young separated refugees aged under 16 in foster care. However, according to a number of social workers and managers there is a national shortage of foster carers and in many areas the shortage of culturally appropriate foster carers, with whom refugee children from those communities of origin can be matched, is especially acute. As a result, foster carers are frequently recruited through private fostering agencies, which pay the carers more than social services do.

The average cost to a local authority for one of their own carers is £217 a week (in inner London this rises to £330).[28] One local authority source in London estimated that the average cost of a private placement is over £500 a week. If more local authority carers were recruited, this would give social services the financial freedom to place more 16- and 17-year-olds in foster care (for these young people the special grant is currently worth up to £300 a week each).

There is a need for more culturally appropriate foster carers to be registered with local authorities to allow social services to fulfil their obligation under the Children Act (1989) to "give due consideration to the child's religious persuasion, racial origin and cultural and linguistic background" (Section 22.5). However, not all separated refugees wish to be placed with foster carers from their country of origin and the Children Act (1989) also requires that a child's wishes be taken into account when making a placement (Section 20.6). For example, two girls told us that they did not want to live with people from their country of origin because they wanted to speak English in the home to improve their language skills. All of the 13 young people we spoke to who had been fostered with English-speakers said one of the good things about living in foster care was that it improved their English. One boy said:

"I could only say 'yes' and 'no' when I arrived. Now I am used to English people."

This aspect of the placement was so important to one boy that he refused a placement on the basis that his proposed carer spoke with a Jamaican accent and he felt this would inhibit his English language development. While we may disagree with his reasoning, this demonstrates the value many young separated refugees place on learning English (see also section 5.7, Education). Only two young people interviewed reported refusing a foster placement on the basis of the carer's suitability. One Christian girl, for example, did not want to live with a Muslim family.

---

[28] Department of Health, *Social Services Performance in 1999-2000* published at www.doh.gov.uk.

Besides language, other good things listed about being in foster care included: getting advice and support, people were nice, holidays and going to school, support with homework and "protection".

Although there is generally more support available to children placed in foster or residential care, both in the home and from a social worker, being in this accommodation can sometimes be seen as a disadvantage by some under-16-year-olds. One boy felt so frustrated living in foster care that as soon as he turned 16 he ran away to stay with friends. When asked about the bad things about being in foster care, young people said: *"it was boring, a small town", "no friends except guy fostered with", "getting used to the food"* and *" I was on my own"*.

A large number of private fostering agencies are based outside London, and consequently their carers generally live outside London. The young people we spoke to who had arrived in London and been placed in foster care outside the city had been eager to return as soon as they turned 16 – even if their experience of foster care was positive – in order to be near their friends. One professional explained that in the London borough where he worked the practice of placing children in foster care outside the area was now avoided, because social workers did not or could not visit the child:

> *"There has been a policy of sending children outside London, which is in line with the government policy of sending adults outside London. There is a problem with that, which is that if you send a child outside of London and their social worker is in London they don't see their social worker."*

Yet in another London authority foster or residential care placements outside of the authority stand at approximately 40 per cent.

5.3.2 Residential homes

"I can't wait for the day I can go from here." (Boy, aged 15)

Separated refugee children are not generally placed in residential homes, but it is not unknown. Eleven of the young people we interviewed had lived in residential care at some time. According to a number of senior social work professionals, this is a budget-led decision. However, the experiences of young refugees who have been placed in residential homes with citizen children suggest that the decision may be fortuitous. In their home countries, most refugee children come under threat from forces outside their own homes; whereas citizen children in public care have often grown up in homes where the threat comes from within.[29] This does not imply life in a residential home is easy for citizen children, only that the children may have different needs. Some professionals have actively resisted

---

[29] Kohli, June 2000.

placing young separated refugees in residential homes for these reasons. One community services manager said:

> *"A rigid care system could create more problems than it solved. I have resisted putting them in care homes. They are overcrowded and have many problems... and they are an unsuitable place for them* [young separated refugees] *to be housed."*

For example, one boy, who had stayed in a home for a month, described some of the other residents as being "in a bad way", and he felt if he had stayed there longer he might have been influenced by them. Another said his experience improved as more time passed but at first he had found it difficult:

> *"Firstly it was not hard... but just strange, you know when you don't understand anything at all, people talking to you. Then I got used to it – it was better then."*

Residential homes appear to be used to accommodate refugee children in the short term while they await a foster placement, or for children "whose behaviour prevents them from being placed with a family", as a social worker said. For example, one girl felt well-suited to living in a residential home.

A 16-year-old girl placed in a foster home believed that she did not receive enough support from her foster carer:

> *"I needed some kind of support but she* [the foster carer] *doesn't care where you are going, you can go anywhere you want. When you come here you have confidence but you get shy and hurt inside. When you go to foster family they should see you as part of the family, they should love you, but you are treated as someone who pays to live."*

After the breakdown of more than one foster placement, social services wanted to place the girl in a bed-and-breakfast. However, she contacted a children's rights organisation which successfully advocated on her behalf for a placement in a residential home. She felt this intervention was crucial in getting a placement where she could feel secure and supported.

In one London borough where under-16s are always placed in accommodation under Section 20, a specialist residential home has been developed as an alternative to scarce foster placements.

Good practice

One borough that has substantial experience in working with separated refugees has found that it is preferable to operate a residential home exclusively for refugees rather than to mix them with citizen children. The refugee children living in this designated home reported a high level of satisfaction with it and there are plans for a second home. Designated homes are said by social workers to offer a "safe haven" for unaccompanied refugees where their needs can be met:

"Their specific cultural needs and needs as an asylum-seeker can be met – for example, dealing with their asylum claim."

According to staff, the aim of the home is to prepare young people for fostering or independent living. In addition, the borough contracts private residential homes outside of the borough for the placement solely of separated refugees.

The homes are intended as short-term placements but young people may be there from one week to six months. When foster placements cannot be found, or there are other exceptional circumstances, young people may stay until they are 18 years old.

One resident of a designated home for separated refugees said:

"It was a very good place, it was the best… They treat us like real family."

Yet the need to individually assess need and monitor placements is reinforced by the comments of another 15-year-old who had lived in the same place:

"You can't build a relationship, they can't look after you like [they] *can in a family because they can't remember what it is from the last time they saw you… A family is much better… this place is temporary and after children should move to a family but they are not quite taking it seriously."*

The bad things referred to by young people were the fact that some link workers were "not friendly to their link child" and did not take their job seriously – indicated by them missing appointments – and the fear and uncertainty surrounding moving on at 16:

"I was told they are looking for semi-independent accommodation, that would be hard for me. I don't know about others, even if I was here [in the residential home] *for three or four years I would not get what I need to be ready for that."*

This comment and other similar comments suggested anxiety among young people preparing for a transition. Others were afraid that they would have to move to independent accommodation that was far from their college and they might have to leave their studies.

The good things listed tended to outweigh the bad and included: staff take you to the doctor and hospital; they get you into a school or college; there are facilities like computers and a TV room; and it is "new and clean" and "people co-operate with each other".

Case study: Joseph

Joseph was fortunate to arrive in a local authority which was well organised and equipped to deal with the needs of young separated refugees. He also arrived at an age which meant he was automatically "looked after". Although he is frustrated by some aspects of his life, his story shows what can happen when arrangements are in place to more fully take into account the needs of young separated refugees.

Joseph has been in the UK for nearly two years. He was 14 years old when he arrived at an airport in the south of England. He was alone and immediately taken into the care of the local authority where the airport was located.

As an emergency measure Joseph was placed in a children's home which is designated for separated asylum-seeking children. However, he ended up staying in the home until he turned 16 because social services were unable to find a suitable foster placement for him. At the home he had a care worker who was responsible for his day-to-day welfare, an allocated social worker and homework support from an education support teacher.

He felt that a foster placement would be better for him than living in a residential home. Nonetheless, he did feel that the place prepared him for life in England and they did look after him. For example, workers ensured he was registered with a doctor and got him as quickly as possible into a local school, where he was making very good progress.

When he turned 16, Joseph was told he would be moved to semi-independent accommodation. He did not feel ready for it but he had no choice. The accommodation was newly refurbished to accommodate about 50 young separated asylum-seekers. Joseph has his own room with a bathroom and small kitchen. There is a communal area and a support worker based at the accommodation 24 hours a day. Joseph no longer has a named social worker or support teacher but he is settled at his new college.

5.3.3 Hostels and private rented accommodation

The term "hostel" encompasses lodgings that are allocated specifically to young separated refugees and also those for homeless citizen young people. Most of the young people we spoke to were living in asylum-seeker-only hostels but in many cases adults were living in unsupervised hostels with minors. The same kind of occupation pattern applies to private rented accommodation, which may be a house of multiple occupation, a bedsit or a bed and breakfast. In all these types of accommodation, conditions were reported, and observed by researchers, to be poor and frequently unsuitable.

CHILD PROTECTION AND APPROPRIATE PLACEMENTS

Six young people talked about events or situations that had occurred in their accommodation that raised particular child protection concerns.[30] In addition, a substantial number of young people were living in inappropriate accommodation. For example, 15 children lived or had lived with adults in unsupervised accommodation, as in the following example.

> Aged 14, one boy had lived in a hostel with 15 other, mostly adult, asylum-seekers for four months. He said:
>
> *"Hostel not too good really, no good at all. Food crap. English people there taking drugs... I was the youngest there, I had some friends my age. Four months at hostel, two [in a] bedroom, shared bathroom... I didn't like it."*
>
> Eventually he was moved out into foster care.

One 14-year-old boy, who was accompanied by a relative and placed in a hostel for asylum-seekers, described why he found the hostel unsuitable:

"It wasn't a suitable place for a child because most of them were old people with mental health problems and [it was] hard to communicate. We were strangers there and very frightened."

Another young boy agreed that a hostel is an unsuitable place for a child:

"If they put you in a hostel or something like that, you can't get on with [your life], because there's lots of bad people in hostel. If you're young boy, child – it's very difficult. I don't think that's a good idea for the young children to take them there."

---

[30] Where appropriate, researchers took steps in line with Save the Children's child protection policy.

In fact, all the young refugees we interviewed who had lived in hostels (24) found it a difficult experience, especially those in homeless hostels where they lived with citizens. One professional reported how two separated refugees, aged 17, had been held in a detention centre as a result of age disputes, and were released to a unit for young people who are vulnerable and at risk:

> *"He came out of a detention centre that he shouldn't have been in anyway, only to land in a house with drug-takers, and his stuff getting nicked."*

The vast majority of social workers thought the practice of placing minors in largely unsupervised settings, such as hostels or shared houses, with adults who have not been assessed for their suitability to live with minors was undesirable; although the practice was recommended on one occasion as a way of helping to support the child. We found some, very limited, evidence that such a placement could prove supportive to a young person. For example, one young boy acted as spokesperson for the other residents of his house and had secured improvements to the accommodation and, in turn, he benefited from living with adults who took care of him sometimes. Nonetheless, this is clearly a high-risk strategy, particularly given the limited support available from social services (see below). It is unlikely that many of these placements are being monitored closely enough to ensure the placement is proving suitable or even safe. Although not all the young people were unhappy about having been housed with adults, it is clear that this practice could raise child protection concerns.

Even where groups of minors are living together there may be child protection concerns. One 16-year-old boy reported being threatened, and added that a housemate used to steal his food until he got a padlock for his cupboard. He said:

> *"A friend of* [a housemate] *came over to the house and put a knife at me and want to have me. He still comes to the house."*

INDEPENDENT VISITORS SCHEMES

Independent monitoring of placements and welfare can be accomplished through the establishment of independent visitors schemes as prescribed in the Children Act (1989). It is obligatory for local authorities to operate these schemes if they believe this would be in the children's best interests, but very few actually do.[31] The independent visitor is intended as an additional measure to safeguard the welfare of children who are isolated from parental contact.[32] Further, the Department of Health guidance on unaccompanied asylum-seeking children states that:

---

[31] See UNHCR/Save the Children, 2000 (2nd ed.), pp. 67–70 for detailed arguments for independent visitors or personal advocates for young separated refugees.

[32] Social Services Inspectorate, 1995: 20.

"It is very likely, given the nature of the situation unaccompanied children find themselves in, that the appointment of an independent visitor will be considered advisable." [33]

None of the young people we spoke to was visited by an independent visitor, although at least one authority had plans to address this.

There are 12 Children's Rights Service projects across the country. One of the services offered is a system of "independent visitors". Our interview with one project leader in Greater Manchester concluded that this could be an important source of social and cultural support. In this project they set out to attract adult befrienders from a variety of cultures, backgrounds, ages and experience. There is potential, with appropriate resources, to develop this service for young separated refugees. This would be linked to assessment under the Children Act (1989), "Quality Protects" and the Children (Leaving Care) Act (2000), and would ensure these children's inclusion in mainstream provision.

CONDITIONS IN HOSTELS AND PRIVATE RENTED ACCOMMODATION

Conditions in both hostels and private rented accommodation were reported to be cramped and lacking basic necessities, and theft was said to be common. One boy described a typical set-up:

"There is not much to tell, a room, I live with some other guy there, I share it with him, not too big, it's got a cooker in the room, a sink, table, plates, two beds… I don't like anything about it at all really. It's too small, we've got the same toilet for everyone that lives in the hostel, there are about six rooms."

The situation of the 17-year-old boy below is typical of the stories of poor conditions and unscrupulous landlords told by many 16- and 17-year-olds placed in private rented accommodation by social services.

One unaccompanied boy was living in a privately rented bedsit which had no hot water or heating for four months during the winter, and was infested with cockroaches. He lived with nine single adults, two of whom he reported were not asylum-seekers, and were alcoholics. His landlord was visited frequently by the police, and the boy believed his landlord might be operating an illegal business from the ground floor of the building.

The boy was advised by a youth worker to contact the Environmental Services Department to report the appalling conditions in the bedsit. After six phone calls someone came to look at the place and took notes, but several months later, nothing had happened. This experience led the boy to question the wisdom of arranging accommodation through private landlords. He asked:

"When [social services] give young people to agencies like private landlords, how do they know what they are like?"

[33] Ibid

These comments about poor conditions fit the with findings of a recent report by the National Campaign for Homeless People, Shelter,[34] based on results collected by environmental health officers in five local authorities. They found that nearly nine out of ten houses of multiple occupation accommodating asylum-seekers were unfit for human habitation, with 80 per cent of them exposed to unacceptable risk of fire. It was also found that people new to this country may be less aware of the risks inherent in unfit housing, such as faulty gas appliances and flammable furniture. In addition, they found that language barriers may lead to delays when evacuating buildings. These problems are worse for children unaccustomed to responsibility for safety of this kind.

The prevalence of poor conditions in the private rented sector increases the need for social services to be alert to problems and available to respond. Clearly, this is made more difficult when young people are placed far from the area the social worker is based.

Good practice
In one of the local authorities researched, the asylum team had a policy of not placing 16- and 17-year-olds outside of the area, which enabled the team to have a 24-hour response time to any complaint from a young separated refugee.

The need for social services to be responsive to problems is further increased by the failure of landlords to respond to problems themselves. This was one of the most frequent complaints from young people about living in private rented accommodation. For example, one boy said he could not get his landlady to carry out repairs:

"Our landlady… said she would do something with the apartment to decorate [it] *but she didn't… Things are not working in the house, like machines, and the landlady says she will do things but she doesn't."*

---

[34] Garvie, 2001.

5.3.4 Semi-independent accommodation

> **Good practice**
> In one local authority a range of excellent semi-independent accommodation
> has been developed, some in conjunction with voluntary organisations, for 16-
> and 17-year-olds. The most recently developed accommodation comprises a
> bathroom, kitchen and bedroom for each of the 50 asylum-seeking residents
> aged 16 or 17. There is a support worker on site 24 hours a day. This set-up
> was very popular with the young people we interviewed living there.

The development of semi-supported accommodation to some extent helps to
compensate for the fact that many 16- and 17-year-olds have very limited access
to care from social workers. Social workers in different parts of the country
expressed a desire for more semi-independent accommodation.

CULTURALLY APPROPRIATE PLACEMENTS

Just as it is important to take cultural considerations into account when making
foster care placements, it is equally important when making all other kinds of
placement (Children Act (1989): Section 22.5). However, a number of
authorities are struggling to accommodate these factors. One social services
director admitted that he had grave concerns about their ability to make
appropriate placements, saying:

> *"We are, on the whole, failing to take account of the ethnic and cultural needs of these
> young people."*

The following examples are evidence of the kinds of culturally inappropriate
placements revealed by our interviews.

> An African boy and his brother live in a small room in a house they share with
> men from eastern Europe. The boy said:
>
> > *"They* [the European men] *don't like* [African] *people. They always want to kick
> > me. I talk to social worker but* [she] *didn't do nothing,* [She] *said, 'You are new so
> > you can't move.'"*
>
> After he had gone to social services every day for a week, a social worker
> agreed to visit him in his flat to discuss the problem with him. The boy stayed
> off college in anticipation of the arranged visit, but no one came.
>
> Another boy reported that he had to share a room with a boy from his
> country, but a different tribe. He had left his country because his tribe were
> fighting people from the other boy's tribe. He told social services he wanted to
> move for this reason. After a month nothing had happened, but when the boys
> started physically fighting they were separated.

5.3.5 Private care and accommodation providers

Where local authorities had entered into contracts with private companies to provide accommodation and care to young separated refugees, living conditions were often worse still. In this situation, local authorities pay an agency to accommodate young separated refugees and take responsibility for facilitating their access to services. However, the local authority retains ultimate responsibility for the young person.

Our research found that private providers were most commonly used by local authorities in the south of England and they tended to be based in the Midlands and the north. This meant the young people placed in the care of private providers were living at considerable distances from the local authority with responsibility for them.

There are three key problems with this practice. First, the appropriateness of the location or type of accommodation seems to play little part in decisions about where to place young people. Second, the quality of accommodation is generally poor and the local environmental services department are rarely able or informed to be able to carry out inspections of the properties. Third, the young people in this situation do not have adequate access to social workers or an independent complaints procedure to improve their accommodation conditions, although they are entitled to both.

Location is important in the sense of both the immediate community and the broader area. It is common for young people to be placed in settings where there is no knowledge or appreciation of their culture, food or language. Although not all the young people had special requirements regarding, for example, religion or food, the lack of appreciation of their cultural needs tended to lead to social isolation. It should not be assumed that young separated refugees will necessarily establish contact with members of the same nationality or religious group who live in the area, since these groups are likely to be cross-cut by different political affiliations or other factors. Even for those practising a religious faith, it cannot be assumed that attending the local mosque or church will be an easy way to get access to broader networks of people.

All these factors need to be taken into account when making an assessment of the appropriateness of a location for the placement for any young person. This, of course, is more difficult for social workers if they do not have the requisite local knowledge when accommodating a young separated refugee outside of their area.

Private agencies that we researched accommodated young separated refugees in areas with a higher-than-average need for social housing (where property prices tend to be lower). In one northern city in particular, the young people said they did not feel safe in the area where they lived. One boy said:

"The house I live in is OK. I just don't like the area where they have housed us. There is a lot of crime. It is not a good area. I don't feel very safe there."

The importance of feeling safe was paramount in the minds of many of the young people we spoke to:

"The best thing about this country is feeling safe…We don't have to live in fear for our lives. We are grateful to be here."

Another boy reported having his bicycle stolen from his house. Harassment in this area seemed to be very common (see 5.8, Social networks).

In one house that we visited we observed that both neighbouring houses were in disrepair and boarded up and it seemed that rubbish had not been collected from the vicinity for some time. Three young people lived in the house, which was a long way from other members of their community and educational institutions. Although the young people were pleased they had been housed with people of their own age, both the house and its contents were in a bad state of repair. It was mice-infested, the furniture was old and damaged, the carpet and walls dirty and smelly and only the bare minimum of household essentials such as knives, forks and glasses had been provided.

One of the young people explained they had tried to secure improvements and informed a teacher about their predicament and she had made a formal complaint to their private provider but, despite promises, nothing had been done:

"We have continually complained to the private provider and they keep promising to do something but nothing ever changes. They are just not interested, we hate living here."

One group of young people had given up on achieving improvements in their accommodation and instead slept on the floor at a friend's house most of the week.

Despite the inadequate accommodation, many young people felt there was a limit to what they were entitled to and could expect. As one participant put it: "I cannot say I want to live in a villa, can I?" However, the UNCRC is clear on the right of children to benefit from an adequate standard of living (Article 27). Further, the Children Act (1989) places a requirement on local authorities to provide children in need with services that grant them a "reasonable standard of health or development" where "'development' means physical, intellectual, emotional, social or behavioural development; and 'health' means physical or mental health" (Section.17.10 and Section 17.11).

Case study: Ali

Ali's story shows what can happen when young unaccompanied refugees are placed in the care of a private agency outside the local authority area with responsibility for them.

Ali is 17 years old and has been placed in the care of a private agency in a small city in the north of England by a local authority in the south. The southern local authority retains legal responsibility for his welfare but the agency is contracted to ensure that his needs are adequately met.

He is not happy living in this city; he says:

> "I did not want to come here but we were not given any choice. I don't like it here. I don't like the people, they are not very friendly."

But more than simply unfriendly, some of his neighbours are also threatening. Ali described one particularly intimidating incident:

> "Two months ago they beat down our door and we were very frightened. Our door is still not fixed but nothing has been done. We sometimes find it difficult to sleep because we are afraid when we hear noises."

Ali lives in a shared house with other young refugees from the same country. The house is overcrowded and in a poor state of repair:

> "I don't like the house I am living in. It is not in very good condition, it's a terrible house. It's cold, dirty, the carpet is old and torn, the washing machine is broken. There are four or five rooms and seven of us living there."

However, both he and the others in the house feel that the agency is no help when it comes to sorting out problems. They said:

> "I have been and complained ten times and no one has come."

> "No one has ever come to visit us since we moved in here [ten months earlier]. The agency are bad. They don't care, they don't help, they don't want to know, there is no point asking them for anything."

Their frustration with their living conditions may be exacerbated by the fact that they have to spend so much time there. Ali tried to enrol on an English course at a college and was told they would get in touch with him – they never did.

His life – and the lives of his housemates – is characterised by unrelenting boredom:

"I get fed up of having nothing to do… We don't hang out with other nationalities. I don't have any English friends. We go into town. Sit around here, go into town. There is nothing to do, it is very boring."

One housemate suggested that this inactivity would eventually affect their health:

"We will eventually go mad. We don't want to sit around, drink cider and cause trouble like a lot of people around here."

Ali concluded our interview saying:

"Don't get me wrong, despite what I have said I am very grateful to be here."

5.4 Support from social workers

"Keep out of trouble and listen to what your social worker tells you as they will know what's good for [you] and what's not." (Boy, aged 17)

Main findings

- The support received by young separated refugees varied greatly. Most "looked after" young separated refugees had some contact with a social worker. Those placed "out of area" were the least likely to have contact with a social worker.

- Private providers appear to be inadequate in facilitating access to services on behalf of social services for young separated refugees.

- Some social services departments are failing to inform other local authorities that they are sending young separated refugees to live in their area.

- Our evidence points to the advantages of supporting young separated refugees through specialist workers within children's services.

- There is a lack of preparedness in the form of strategic planning, local networking and information sharing in relation to young separated refugees in many areas.

- Social workers pointed to a need for training in working with interpreters and in cultural awareness.

Key factors affecting level of support received from social workers:
- What level of contact exists between the young person and social services and do they have an allocated social worker?
- How is social service provision to young separated refugees in the area organised?
- Is there strategic planning of services to young separated refugees?
- What is the ratio of social workers to young people?
- How much experience and training do staff have of working with young separated refugees?

5.4.1 Level of contact

"No one cares about us. My social worker asked me once what I wanted, but it was right at the beginning and I didn't know anything then." (Boy, aged 16)

The level of contact a young separated refugee had with a social worker was frequently critical in determining whether a young person had their basic rights fulfilled. Among the young people we spoke to, the level of contact varied from no contact at all, to regular and constructive meetings between the young person and social worker.

"LOOKED AFTER" CHILDREN

Young refugees in the "looked after" system had mixed experiences of support from social workers but all at least had some knowledge of a social worker's role. The majority of all those young people who said they had a social worker (36 out of 53) said they saw their social worker only when they had a problem and most relied on their carers for day-to-day support. However, this group clearly had more experience of social workers than young separated refugees in other support arrangements.

Some "looked after" children reported having to wait up to three months to be allocated a social worker while others reported having a series of temporary workers before they got their own social worker.

The young people's responses to social workers ranged from a sense of resignation that they do not have either the will or the power to do much, to a deep sense of appreciation:

"Social services just do the work, they aren't gonna help you."

"Their problem is they listen but no answers."

"They are 100 per cent helpful – all of them… wow, that's good!"

However, most young people who did have regular contact with a social worker clearly felt they benefited from it and felt they would benefit from more frequent meetings in recognition that their needs change over time.

"From social services we need more visits, more regular. They come the first time when you move into a house, you can't think what your needs are straight away. If they came regularly then you would know what you need all the time."

CHILDREN UNDER SECTION 17 (NOT "LOOKED AFTER")

In one region, 21 out of 36 young people accommodated under Section 17 did not have access to a named social worker. It was common for professionals in the statutory sector to say that social services were providing a very limited, accommodation-focused service to these young people:

> *"Social services provide a roof and food that is all. Some help with school, some don't. They are not providing the social back-up that young separated refugees desperately need."*

The majority of young people reported that they saw a social worker when they went to their office to collect money or when they had a problem. It was rare for a young person to report that social workers visited them in their accommodation. Although there are practical reasons why this may be the case, it does significantly diminish the ability of the social worker to assess needs and respond to and pre-empt problems.

CHILDREN UNDER SECTION 17 AND PLACED "OUT OF AREA" WITH A PRIVATE PROVIDER

> *"I get the feeling that social services are not treating them specially enough and taking responsibility. They can go back and forth, passing the buck, avoiding, trying to get away with the least possible."* (Professional)

The ultimate responsibility for the care of young people who are placed outside of the area with a private provider remains with social services. However, the day-to-day care of the young person was sometimes also contracted out to the company providing the accommodation. Whether or not care was contracted out, young people living out of area in private rented accommodation had minimal, if any, contact with social workers. Instead they got support, where they could, from their contemporaries or teachers.

Social services departments have a duty to notify the social services department of the receiving authority when they place a "looked after" young person in their area (in accordance with the Children Act 1989, Regulation 5). In the case of children who are not "looked after", it is considered good practice to notify the receiving authority but it was common for agencies in receiving authorities to report that sending social services departments were failing to do this.

In two local authorities in the north of England, none of those interviewed realised that they were under the care of a local authority in the south nor, indeed, what this meant. They did not understand the term social worker and did not realise they could obtain help if in need. They saw their only point of contact as the private provider. Importantly, they felt that the private providers were inadequate in this respect. For example, one boy who had been in the "care" of a private provider for ten months confirmed that he had received little attention:

"No one has ever come to visit us since we moved in here."

The young people expected private providers to be either unresponsive or inadequately responsive to their requests for help. In one area 12 out of 17 of the young people whose care was "contracted out" complained that their private landlord had provided an interpreter only when they first arrived, that information was rushed and the written information provided was in English. In this area all those whose care was contracted out expressed the belief that the providers would not be interested in helping them. All were unaware of how to make a complaint. One young separated refugee explained:

"They are only interested in the money they can make out of us. They are not interested in our problems. We are only a business for them."

Under the terms of most contracts[35] private providers are required to facilitate access to services such as doctors, dentists and schools and to provide young people with information on health, education, leisure, recreation, legal provision and the police. However, in one area, for example, 13 out of 18 young people told us they had found out about education and leisure provision by word of mouth rather than from their provider.

In the absence of significant support from either a social worker or private provider, one young person had gained support through a voluntary organisation:

"Occasionally the social worker comes up but it is very, very rare; in fact this person has only seen us twice. My only real support has been at the local community advice centre. I don't know where I would be without him helping me out."

Few of the young people interviewed felt that the private provider responsible for facilitating their care could be trusted. For example, one young person interviewed had health and housing problems, and when the researcher offered to ask the provider for help on his behalf, he said he was worried that if she did so, they "might send me home".

In one area we found evidence of a provider taking their responsibilities more seriously, and in this instance the staff did visit the young people and offered some support:

"We support them by going round, visiting them, seeing they're all right, making sure the house is OK, talking through any problems they have, help them with solicitors, doctors, hospitals, whatever it may be. And that's just a daily thing. And... the office area is used as like a general meeting place... and... they come in to claim their allowance here and that's the time they flag the issues." (Private provider staff)

---

[35] See Garvie, 2001 on the use of "commercial confidentiality" to protect many such contracts from public scrutiny.

Social services in the areas where the private providers are located expressed concern that other local authorities had sent separated refugees to the area without informing any local agencies. A number of workers suggested that this meant that the sending authority was not fulfilling its responsibility towards these young people:

"In a lot of cases… they [the sending authority] *just did deals with landlords here… people were just put on a bus and met by a private landlord and put in a flat… nobody even knew they were here."* (Health worker)

"I've been very concerned that there are unaccompanied minors in [area] *that were dispersed by* [another local authority] *and* [authority has] *consistently failed in their duty of care for those unaccompanied minors."* (Social services worker)

Given the needs of these young people, serious questions must be asked about the appropriateness of arranging the provision of care from a distance of as much as 300 miles from the physical location of the local authority with responsibility for that care.

5.4.2 Organisation of support: a child-centred or asylum-centred team?

"We are treated as second-class workers in a second-class team serving what are considered second-class children." (Social worker)

The way a local authority organises the provision of services and support to young separated refugees will affect the experiences of the young people. The three most important aspects of this organisation are the structure of the teams, the ratio of social workers to young people and the level of training and experience in the team.

In the areas we researched social services departments organise the provision of services to unaccompanied asylum-seeking children in one of three main ways:

- specialist asylum social workers or non-specialist social workers based in children's services

- asylum team working with unaccompanied children as well as families and single adults, located in the housing department or social services

- a combination of the above with under-16s in the care of children's services and 16- and 17-year-olds in the care of an asylum team.

WORKING WITHIN CHILDREN'S SERVICES

There is a considerable range of opinion about the organisational approach that best serves the interests of young separated refugees. Our evidence clearly points to the advantages of supporting them through specialist workers in children's services, as this leads to them being seen as children first and receiving a full needs assessment while their particular needs as asylum-seekers are also appreciated. Seven (out of 13) of the local authorities we looked at had already organised or were considering organising their service in this way.

It was argued by social workers that if the specialist asylum team was working within children's services, the staff were plugged into discussions and developments in childcare generally, and this provided the opportunity to promote the fair treatment of asylum-seeking children. There was a strong link between young people reporting a positive and fruitful relationship with their social worker and the existence of a specialist asylum team within children's services.

Where young separated refugees are the responsibility of children's services in which there are no specialist asylum workers, according to one social worker they get lost among potentially more demanding citizen children:

> *"My experience tells me that in a busy caseload when you've got court deadlines, where you have got a lot of very demanding, damaged children and you have got an asylum-seeker, the asylum-seeker will take very much second place because they are not making any demands. They are going to school, they are not causing you problems, they are not demanding and they are just a case."*

This was a view held across sectors and across the country. Further, it was argued that non-specialist children's services teams are in effect largely concerned with child protection, so that before a service can be offered, a "risk" assessment is carried out. On the one hand this means the assessment is thorough but the categorisation of a child "in need" as being in need of "child protection" is misleading and potentially unhelpful in terms of meeting the needs of young separated refugees. Moreover, this way of working may distort official statistics of child protection investigations. It is a short-term solution, and some rethinking is needed in the long term, including a clearer pathway for young separated refugees through the system within mainstream provision, and increased resources directed towards appropriate assessment and support.

WORKING WITHIN AN ASYLUM TEAM

The second type of structure is to have an asylum team which works with separated children, single adults and families. In cases where this structure had been adopted, even if those within the team were clear that these children had distinct and additional rights and needs as children, in the eyes of those outside the team, the young people were viewed as asylum-seekers first and as young people second. This led to difficulty in obtaining services and resources from other parts of a social services department, because the young people, regarded as asylum-seekers, were thus seen as the responsibility of the asylum team. This kind of attitude was partly accounted for by familiar issues of workload and resources, and partly driven by a belief that the young people in question were not really under 18 years old.

WORKING DIFFERENTLY WITH UNDER-16s AND OVER-16s

The third structure divides responsibility for young separated refugees according to their age. This approach may be influenced by the grant structure which pays less for the support of 16- and 17-year-olds than it does for the under-16s. The division pre-supposes the kind of support that a young person will require based on their age. In one area responsibility for 16- and 17-year-olds had been transferred to the asylum team within the housing department. This was done in order to improve access to accommodation but, although the measure secured improved accommodation for this age group, the transfer of responsibility was not accompanied by the transfer of adequate social work staff, and the young people in this area were keenly aware of the limits to the social work support they could expect.

5.4.3 Strategic planning and staff resources: "learning as we go along"

"They [refugees] *are experiencing difficulties because of displacement, difficulties to settle in, all that kind of stuff. I don't believe for the most part that the standard trained social worker in Britain has been given training… to deal with those situations."* (Social services professional)

Some social workers in all areas, but especially in areas where they have only recently started to support young separated refugees, felt that they were insufficiently supported and trained to work with this group. In fact, some had little knowledge of the legislation or the immigration status of the young people they supervised. Furthermore, the resources available to them were often very limited and they were forced to look for appropriate support elsewhere, such as within the education system and voluntary sector. Many professionals put this down to a lack of strategic planning. In addition, there appears to be a national shortage of social workers and difficulties in recruitment and retention.

Many social workers complained about a lack of guidance, despite the existence of the comprehensive 1995 Department of Health practice guide:

"There was no information… To this day I've still got very little formal written stuff or guidelines; we create our own guidelines and we've kind of sussed out what other people's

ideas were and then found a position within all those, because invariably we get three different positions from… three different people… There was no preparation, there was no forward information."

This kind of lack of preparedness was described in many areas outside London. The evidence gathered from our research suggests that a lack of preparedness was not simply due to the unpredictable nature of arrivals, given that year on year the numbers of unaccompanied minors continue to rise, albeit at an unpredictable rate. Instead it appears to be the result of unwillingness by local authorities to recognise that the support of young separated refugees is a long-term issue. This means setting up effective organisational structures and creating capacity, including young separated refugees in strategic planning, and investing in staff.

In some areas local authorities have been slow to create capacity to address the needs of refugees. For example, one health worker told us she was the first person with a remit to look at the health needs of refugees at a time when there were already 1,000 refugees in the area and she was "starting from scratch".

When managers do recognise the need for more staff to work with young separated refugees there are frequently difficulties in recruitment, particularly in the light of the national shortage of social workers. In the areas we looked at, social workers tended to have heavy caseloads, the heaviest being one social worker to over 300 young separated refugees. In one London borough we looked at, social workers in the leaving care team, who work with both refugee and citizen children, had a more manageable caseload of 20 each.

Good practice

There are now some clear devices for achieving strategic planning: for example, through Quality Protects management action plans, which all local authorities are required to produce, and children's services plans. One former social services manager recommends Quality Protects as a way of improving services for young separated refugees:

"If we can align these separated children with the spirit of Quality Protects, they would benefit from our efforts to promote social inclusion, avoid expensive failures, and work in holistic ways with partner agencies." (Little, 2001)

Since one of the regional reports of the present project was circulated, the lead officers responsible for strategic planning for children have committed themselves to writing a new chapter in both their current Quality Protects management action plan and their children's services plan to address the needs of young separated refugees.

Quality Protects (see box above) does not include specific indicators for young separated refugees, although the development of such indicators could encourage a greater number of local authorities to incorporate this group more effectively into their planning and service delivery.

By mid-2000 only 12 per cent of all local authorities had a refugee strategy[36] although the introduction of the Home Office strategy for refugee integration[37] may provide the impetus for more local authorities to develop such plans. However, the Home Office strategy targets only those who have leave to remain, and excludes those who have yet to receive a decision.

The lack of strategic thinking is reflected at both local and national level in the absence of centrally held, current and accessible data. On a local and regional level, this data is necessary not only to support applications for support grants, but also to develop a picture of this group of asylum-seekers as part of an assessment of their needs. On a national level this data is needed if an informed strategic approach to meeting the needs of young separated refugees is to be adopted.

The lack of preparedness and strategic thinking are linked with a lack of local networking and information-sharing. Frustration with the lack of inter-agency communication was common:

> *"Part of the problem with* [this area] *is that there are lots of different people working with asylum-seekers and not really communicating what it is they're doing."* (Social services worker)

A social worker working with young separated refugees can find their role quickly becomes "a blended version of being a lawyer, an immigration officer, a therapist, a carer, a teacher and a doctor".[38] Clearly a high level of skills is necessary to fulfil the demands of such a role. Social workers pointed to a particular need for training in working with interpreters and in cultural awareness, which is crucial in making appropriate placements.

This combination of a lack of training and experience and inadequate infrastructure and resources led a number of social workers to conclude that they were offering a less-than-adequate service to young separated refugees:

> *"The unaccompanied minors we deal with probably get 25 per cent of the service that I think I'd be able to offer immediately to a young person in the indigenous population."* (Social services worker)

---

[36] Audit Commission, 2000.

[37] Home Office, 2001.

[38] Kohli, June 2000.

5.5 Financial support

Main findings

- The amount of financial support received by the young separated refugees varied depending on local authority practice and their care status.

- "Looked after" young separated refugees were generally more satisfied with the level of financial support they received. However, those who were not "looked after" were less satisfied.

- Six local authorities we looked at issued vouchers or a combination of vouchers and cash to 16- and 17-year-old asylum-seekers, and the young people were very restricted as to how they could spend the vouchers.

- In one area young separated refugees placed in full-board accommodation were not given any financial support at all, which could cause severe hardship.

Key factors affecting financial support received by a young person:
- Is the young person "looked after" or not?
- Does the local authority provide financial support in vouchers or cash?
- Does the local authority exercise discretion in a clear and transparent way?

5.5.1 "Looked after" children

Young separated refugees who were "looked after" were supported through cash payments of pocket money via their carer or key worker. Most of the young people we spoke to were satisfied with the money they received and the activities this enabled them to do.

Good practice

In one London borough all "looked after" children receive £200 emergency clothing allowance on entering the care of the authority; thereafter they receive £35 a month for clothing and toiletries, £274 in their first year of school for school clothes and £83 a year for the following years. These amounts are paid to the carer to be passed on to the child at their discretion and are the same as the amounts received by citizen children.

In other places the practice varies widely and some young people living together noted the discrepancy in what they received:

"My social worker gives me whatever I ask for."

"But I asked for money from my social worker for books but never got any."

Young people aged 16 and 17 who have been "looked after" but have moved into semi-independent or independent accommodation receive cash payments. The amounts vary from place to place, from £26 to £31.95 a week. Young people often felt the amount was insufficient, especially to buy clothes as well as food:

"When I first got my £27 I did not know what to buy at the supermarket… with £27 you can't do very much."

However, these young people frequently had the benefit of a relationship with a social worker to whom they could go if they had financial problems. In most cases social workers were able to respond with one-off payments, for example, to buy crockery or a winter coat. Two boys reported such an instance:

"Once we told him [our social worker] *that the money is not enough and he found some things for us like bedding and stuff."*

5.5.2 Children under Section 17

LOCAL AUTHORITY VOUCHERS

Seven of the thirteen local authorities we looked at supported 16- and 17-year-old separated refugees with cash; five gave them a combination of cash and vouchers and one gave just vouchers. These vouchers should not be confused with the NASS-issued vouchers given to asylum-seeking adults and families. Local authorities are required to support with vouchers all asylum-seeking adults and families who arrived after April 2001 and before NASS took over responsibility for asylum-seekers in their area. Some local authorities have chosen to extend this scheme to separated 16- and 17-year-olds, although this is not government policy.

Those young people we interviewed who received local authority vouchers (15) described how these restricted what they could do and how they affected their lives. The vouchers are not accepted on public transport. One effect of this is that the young people must be able to walk to college, which creates particular difficulties for young people with physical disabilities.

> One unaccompanied 17-year-old we spoke to had a disability that meant he could only walk with the help of crutches. He had to walk between his hostel and college every day because he received vouchers, which could not be used on public transport.
>
> In addition, the vouchers were not accepted in the college. He did not receive a packed lunch and did not eat all day until he returned to the hostel for dinner. He described the situation:
>
> *"Eight o'clock get up, four o'clock go home – no food."*

One senior professional suggested that vouchers were issued to 16- and 17-year-olds on the grounds that their needs were similar to those of adults. This thinking is not in line with the legislation relating to children, which stresses the requirement for a full needs-led assessment of every child, defined as someone under 18 years. Furthermore, the vouchers given to 16- and 17-year-olds are often more restricted in their use than the NASS-issued vouchers given to many adults. For example, in one area the vouchers that are issued can be spent only in two national supermarket chains. This means that the young people cannot shop in the markets, cheaper shops or stores selling culturally appropriate products.

NO FINANCIAL SUPPORT

The research found that in two areas young people placed in full-board accommodation are not given any financial support at all. This can cause a multitude of hardships, one of the most obvious being when a young person is at college and is not provided with a packed lunch, so cannot eat all day. Two young people described the restrictions that result from receiving neither cash nor vouchers:

> *"I cannot buy clothes, get my hair cut, travel by bus, buy a bottle of water or just go to the toilet. I had to borrow money from my stepbrother to get to the Home Office interview."*

> *"You need money to do anything in this country. Since I arrived here every day has been the same, sometimes I feel so angry I don't eat but just go to bed."*

Save the Children believes those young separated refugees who receive no cash or vouchers are being denied their rights under the UNCRC – particularly Articles 27 (the right to an adequate standard of living) and 31 (the right to leisure, recreation and cultural activities). It could be argued that this practice may be vulnerable to challenge under the Human Rights Act, Article 3, which states that everyone has a right to freedom from torture, inhuman and degrading treatment.

CASH

Of those who received cash, most thought the amount was insufficient or only just enough. Some found it hard to keep up with bill payments. Buying food was the major outgoing for most young people we spoke to and frequently this left them no money for buying clothes or a bus pass:

> *"I have not got a change of clothes. Money is not sufficient. I have not got a toothbrush because I have to buy food. I walked to the interview because I have no bus pass... I need to wash my clothes and put them back on."*

A lack of money was acutely felt by young people living in rural areas where they needed to pay for transport in order to get access to any services or attend college.

The financial support for young refugees placed outside of the area with responsibility for them is the same as for those 16- and 17-year-olds accommodated within the local authority. However, the lack of monitoring of these placements means that the system can fail to work effectively.

One 17-year-old boy was living in private rented accommodation at some distance from the local authority with responsibility for him. The local authority paid the private provider an amount each week to be passed on to him for his subsistence.

It was the boy's understanding that the money should be passed on to him in cash. However, his landlord gave him supermarket gift vouchers in place of cash. The boy said he felt he was being treated like an animal.

It is important to note that issues concerning financial support, and care and accommodation in general, do not stop when a young person is granted leave to remain. Their entitlements will then be the same as those for citizen children but they will not necessarily have a smooth transition from one status to another. For example, one boy aged 14 – accompanied by his brother – described a flawed process:

> *"The payment was stopped when we had the asylum decision. One month-and-a-half owed in back payment... They promised they would get us a flat, a permanent place, but so far nothing has come through."*

5.6   Transition at 18 years

"I will have a hard time in the future, I am really worried... You are not a normal person, you are not settled down. You have to be ready to do that. My mum wouldn't do that." (Girl, aged 16)

Main findings

- **There is considerable confusion, anxiety and a lack of information about what happens to a young person when they reach 18 years.**

- **A number of professionals pointed to the potentially disastrous effects of the transition to adult systems at 18, especially dispersal, which entails the loss of friends, support and even homelessness.**

Key factors affecting a young person's transition to adult services at 18 years:
- Is clear information provided to them about what happens at 18?
- Are they "looked after" or not? If they are, they are likely to be entitled to leaving care services and unlikely to be dispersed. If they are not, they are likely to be dispersed.

5.6.1   Lack of information

"I heard I will have problems at 18." (Girl, aged 16)

There was considerable confusion and anxiety among young people about what would happen when they reached 18. Therefore we also spoke to 29 young people aged 18 or over, to gain some understanding of the experience of this transition.

When 17-year-olds were asked what they thought would happen when they turned 18, they replied:

"Money will be stopped and the contribution to accommodation will be halved."

"Everything stops at 18... If you want to get money for travel you can't."

"I don't know. I think it will change from social services to social security, but I'm not sure."

One young person on the brink of 18 had been provided with some information but clearly felt uncertain about how he would cope:

"I have to leave the place I am now when I am 18, and if I can't get a house or permanent flat from the housing department, I have to find a house by myself and that makes it a bit difficult for me... Many people want to work for themselves not to get from DSS, but they are scared of housing because it is expensive, £130 per week, and you can't get a job to cover £130."

5.6.2 NASS dispersal

If a young person's immigration status is unresolved they will be transferred to NASS for support (if they applied for asylum after NASS took over responsibility for asylum-seekers in the area where they made their application) and may be dispersed to another part of the country when they turn 18 years.

NASS disperses asylum-seekers to wherever it has accommodation, which means that a young person may be dispersed even if they are already living in one of the dispersal areas outside the south-east. NASS has stated that it will take into account "exceptional circumstances" when judging whether or not to disperse an individual. For example, it is unlikely to disperse immediately a young person who is about to take public examinations.[39] In addition, recent guidance states that NASS will not ordinarily seek to disperse young people who have been "looked after" when they turn 18 years.[40] However, there is considerable confusion among social workers and other professionals about precisely what would constitute "exceptional circumstances".

It was argued by many professionals we spoke to that the dispersal of former unaccompanied minors at 18 would be disastrous. One teacher said it would be bad for young people because it would take them away from their communities and colleges:

"They've got their communities, that's the only stability they've got in their life apart from their college, and they do rely on college a lot, it's their social life, it's their one chance to get on."

Another suggested young asylum-seekers might go underground for fear of being dispersed – which would make already vulnerable children much more so. She described how this has already started to happen as NASS try to disperse children in families:

"What can happen is that they get so worried about that happening [dispersal] that they disappear, off all lists, everything, they stop coming to college because they think that would be a key to where they are and they will just get jobs working under the table."

---

[39] NASS Policy Bulletin 29, October 2000.

[40] Department of Health, Children (Leaving Care) Act (2000) guidance, 2001.

Further research is required to look more closely at the experiences of young asylum-seekers when they turn 18 and make the transition to NASS, especially in the light of sharp criticism of the principle of dispersal.

Those who arrived before NASS assumed responsibility in the area where they are living will not be transferred to NASS but will continue to be supported by the local authority. Nonetheless, they will also have to go through a testing transition to the adult system. They will face an accommodation move and receive voucher, rather than cash, support.

When young refugees are moved on from hostels or other independent accommodation, because either they have turned 18, or they have been granted leave to remain, they may be given just two weeks' notice before being required to leave the hostel and apply for alternative housing and support. This can leave them homeless and without income while they make new arrangements. One education professional said:

> *"It's a complete disaster when that happens. They are just out on the street if they haven't got friends."*

The experience of three young refugees reported by a voluntary housing advice organisation (below) illustrates the problems for young refugees approaching their 18th birthday with unresolved asylum status.

Aged 16 and speaking minimal English, three unaccompanied boys were told by the social services team responsible for them that they must find their own privately rented accommodation and social services would pay for it, up to a certain amount. The three boys arrived in London before April 2000, so they were entitled to housing benefit and income support, rather than being transferred to NASS for support.

Remarkably – despite their lack of English language, contact networks and local knowledge – they did find a flat. However, they were offered no pastoral support from social services, and perhaps not surprisingly they were soon in trouble with the landlord for having friends to stay. They were served with an eviction order. By the time the order goes to court, the boys will be aged over 18 and no longer the responsibility of social services. None of them has received a decision on his asylum application. It will soon be down to the boys to prove to the housing department that they are homeless, in order to find new accommodation.

A housing advice organisation requested copies of the needs assessments (completed under the requirements of the Children Act 1989) for the boys in January 2000, in order to challenge their treatment. By December 2000 they had still not received them.

5.7 Education

"The only important thing is education." (Boy, aged 17)

Main findings

- Young separated refugees and professionals alike emphasised the importance of their participation in education but many young people aged 16 and 17 living outside of London, and those who were not "looked after", were unable to get a place in full-time education.

- Schools and colleges need more support and resources to cope with the needs of refugee children.

- The Ethnic Minority and Traveller Achievement Grant (EMTAG) is regarded as a valuable resource by professionals, and young people rated highly the service they received from English support teachers. However, the level of support varied from area to area and it was severely over-stretched in some areas.

- The grant of £500 per student made for some asylum-seeking children supported through NASS is welcome but is very limited in its scope.

- Nearly one third of young people interviewed reported racist bullying and harassment, some of which took place in school or college.

Key factors affecting a young person's satisfaction with education services:

- Is appropriate education available and readily accessible?
- Is the school/college/social services/carer prepared to provide extra support, in terms of:
  - English language
  - pastoral care
  - financial support?
- Is there a positive attitude among teachers and other students towards refugees?

5.7.1 Access to appropriate education

"I just sit around and watch TV all the time, but I want to study all the time." (Boy, aged 17)

Figure 7: Table to show young separated refugees in education

	School	College – full-time	College – part-time	Not in education
Young people attending	24	34	27	31

ASSESSMENT

Local authorities have a legal duty to meet the educational needs of all young people of statutory education age living in their area (see Chapter 3, The policy context). Young people aged 16 and 17 are entitled to have access to learning, and social workers and careers guidance professionals should support them to enrol on appropriate courses. However, it is clear from our research that social workers and education professionals do not always work together to ensure a young person has a place on a suitable educational course, particularly when the young person is placed outside of the local authority area where their social worker is based. In those cases where there is close inter-agency working between social and education services, the young person does benefit.

> **Good practice**
> Personal education plans (PEPs – see Chapter 3, The policy context) can be used to ensure that the educational needs of "looked after" children are met. PEPs are not yet widely used in the local authorities we researched, although in one area they have been used for over a year in a residential home for refugees and there are plans to extend their use to children in foster homes.
>
> The PEP is based on the following principles:
> - Give priority to meeting the young person's educational needs, even where these are compounded by other severe problems.
> - Ensure that the educational rights of the young person are safeguarded, and that appropriate educational and community resources are made available to them.
>
> One education professional who uses PEPs said the aim was to get people working together:
>
> > *"The whole point is that "looked after" children, the schools and children's homes are acting together as parents jointly; it's a joint responsibility… It is a way of making sure there is a discussion."*
>
> A PEP can help determine the most appropriate school or college for a young person to attend.

The importance of addressing educational needs in a young separated refugee's needs assessment was reinforced by the experiences of a number of young people who felt they had not had access to any particularly helpful or appropriate education:

> *"When I came first I went to the high school for three months… It was too hard for me, I didn't speak any English so it was too hard… for someone who doesn't speak any English at all it wasn't helpful. I need*[ed] *more time* [before going there].*"*

> *"They put me with smaller* [children]*, younger than me and I couldn't handle that… I couldn't stay there, it is like I was the oldest of all, it wasn't nice. I had some arguments with some pupils… most of the time I stood by myself."*

These early negative experiences of school put these boys off pursuing a place at college later.

ACCESS TO EDUCATION

Usually through adult support in the case of under 16-year-olds and through ingenuity, luck or occasionally adult support in the case of 16- and 17-year-olds, most young separated refugees are able to get on to some kind of educational course.

There was a marked difference, regarding access to full-time, appropriate education with adequate English language support for young people of all ages, between the areas of London we looked at and those we looked at elsewhere. In London all the young people we spoke to who wanted to be in education were on a course and all were at least reasonably happy with the provision. This contrasts with the picture in other parts of the country. In the other areas approximately 38 per cent of young people were known not to be in education and nearly 50 per cent of those in college were on part-time courses. The majority of those on part-time courses wanted to be on full-time courses. Young people were chiefly interested in English language, information technology and vocational courses, including medicine and engineering.

It appears that in London the long history of providing education to children for whom English is not their first language means that there is greater availability of places. However, in other areas EMTAG (see below) is under intense pressure to fund and guide schools, as the services it funds are the only agencies with significant experience of providing the kind of English language support required. In many places colleges have been slow to react to the needs of young separated refugees, although those which do run specific courses tend to be rated highly.

> **Good practice**
> At a London hostel run by the Refugee Council for 16- and 17-year-olds, support staff work with all residents to help them to enrol in the most appropriate institution and course, and then follow up to ensure the young person is attending. Support staff also try to help with homework.
>
> If the young person does not want to go to school, college or an adult education centre, they will be referred to a careers adviser and a local volunteer may be recruited to come in and help them with their English. According to a support worker, the results speak for themselves:
>
> *"Most residents – about 90 per cent – are doing very well academically."*

Furthermore, those young separated refugees who were "looked after" appeared better able to get access to education than those who were living independently or semi-independently. Nevertheless, "looked after" young people placed "out of area" with access to a social worker (eg, in foster care) can also face difficulties. Foster carers and social workers have a joint responsibility to ensure the young person in their care is attending a school suitable to their needs. However, in practice, social workers, as several of them admitted, may not have the local knowledge or contacts to be able to play their part in this process; and then, as one said, it comes down to the carer:

"The foster carer is the starting point, but if they end up with a good school it is down to luck."

Nonetheless, the additional support provided by carers and social workers to "looked after" children usually ensures that the young person is in education within a reasonable period. All of the 21 children we interviewed who were currently "looked after" were in full-time education.

In contrast, in our research, those placed "out of area" in semi-independent or independent accommodation frequently had to rely on their own initiative and luck to secure a place in education. They suffered from the failure of either social services and/or private providers to facilitate access to education. In cases where the responsibility for facilitating access to services had been transferred to the private provider, social services frequently failed to monitor the providers. For these young people, getting a place in education depended on the local infrastructure for assisting refugees into education (eg, a refugee education support worker), the availability of places and chance. In some places where "out of area" placements were being made the local infrastructure was very limited, for example, in Yorkshire and Humberside.

One boy ended up on a college course that he found very unsatisfactory because it was only two days a week. He could have enrolled on a different course but a lack of adult support prevented him from achieving this:

"I was aware of another course at college but because of my limited understanding of English, I didn't understand the right date, where I had to go and what exactly I had to do, [so] *I just missed the beginning."*

In some areas local initiatives have ensured there is some kind of support to help young separated refugees into education. For example, in one city a school settlement officer works with separated refugee children as well as those in families, to help them into education and to get maximum benefit from it. The officer has a caseload of 420 families and over 30 young separated refugees, with referrals coming through local housing agents. In effect, this officer is taking on the responsibilities of other local authorities placing young separated refugees "out of area". While it is the responsibility of the host local education authority to educate all minors living in its area, the sending local authority is responsible for facilitating access to education as part of their responsibility to that child. Clearly, this kind of arrangement has resource implications for the host authority, which funds the post of school settlement officer. This particular officer noted that the role was made more difficult by the lack of communication and co-ordination between and even within the authorities concerned:

"I think it is ludicrous that nobody seems to know how many people are coming to [local authority]. We can have NASS sending them to become [local authority's] responsibility. We can have NASS sending them through a housing agent. And then we can have London boroughs sending them as well, and there is no co-ordination. When you are dealing with people's lives why isn't there any communication? You are trying to meet the needs but you don't know how many you're trying to meet the needs for."

Good practice

We identified some schools, but particularly colleges, that took a proactive approach to encouraging landlords and social workers to inform the young people about their courses. For example, one college made it as straightforward as possible for young separated refugees to enrol. They told the private provider to give the young people a letter confirming they were asylum-seekers receiving basic financial support.

ACCESS TO FULL-TIME EDUCATION

Some statutory school-aged refugee children and many aged over 16 are not getting a full-time education.

When he was 15 years, one boy attended English language classes – along with two other refugees – for two hours a day, but he would have liked more classes. He said:

"I want to have more lessons, English is the most important thing to get right."

The boys were not asked to join the mainstream curriculum classes. By the end of one month at the school all three boys had turned 16 and they were asked to leave the school. The boy we interviewed went to a voluntary organisation for advice.

Given that he had received only one month's English language tuition, his English was still at a very low level. He could have stayed on at the school if there were suitable 6th form courses, but staying on to do English only was not an available option. The Learning Gateway offers provision for "all those disengaged from learning" which is tailored to their individual needs. However, the boy was not informed about this provision. The only option presented to him was to do four to six hours a week of English as a Second or Other Language (ESOL) classes provided by the adult education department.

Young people generally felt that learning English on a part-time basis was unsatisfactory and full-time education would have helped them:

> *"The other possibility that would have helped, would have been making it like a whole week course, rather than only two days a week, because what I have learned in two days I completely forget in the rest of the week. It was very difficult."*

Frequently the only place that young separated refugees get the opportunity to learn English is in the formal setting of the school or college because few have English friends outside these settings who they can talk with (see 5.8, Social networks). Furthermore, attending school or college on a part-time basis does nothing to improve their chances of making English friends.

It is the responsibility of the school to ensure that all children on its roll attend classes on a full-time basis. One education professional felt the lack of full-time provision could be addressed by social workers reporting this to EMTAG staff or an education officer. However, it should be noted that social workers have reported difficulties when attempting to address problems with educational provision in certain schools.

5.7.2 English language support

"I would like to learn perfect English. English is a skill for the future." (Boy, aged 17)

IN SCHOOL

Once in a school or college, most of the young people we interviewed began an English language course. At school this usually meant taking some lessons outside of mainstream classes with a specialist English teacher funded through EMTAG. At college its usually meant enrolling on an ESOL course. While the great majority of the young people we spoke to felt that the quality of this provision was high, as we have seen, many would have liked more hours per week.

Education professionals in four areas reported that the schools that were experienced in working with refugees were by then full. It is increasingly important for these schools to share their experience and practice with other schools that are less accustomed to accommodating the needs of refugee students.

When young refugees participate in mainstream classes it can prove a challenge to the student and teacher, perhaps as a result of the student's limited English language ability or their educational history. Some teachers, however, felt that it was preferable for refugee children to be educated in mainstream classes. One school settlement officer said that teaching refugee children in separate classes generated "intrigue and interest, that those children must be different".

One group of girls who had participated in mainstream classes since starting school here aged 14 or 15 had found it a culture shock. Two others, however, felt more comfortable in class because they were not the only foreign students. One said:

"I think what made it easier for us in this school, rather than any other, is there [were]... many foreign students in this school and they would, like, empathise with your situation. Like when you couldn't speak English or couldn't pull the words out of your mouth, they... wouldn't get tired and just turn their back on you... Because it's not only English students or mostly English students, it's just mixed... I think it was much easier for us because of that."

This comment indicates the difficulties facing students and teachers in areas where there is no substantial history of multiculturalism. One response to this challenge has been to place refugees in classes with children with other special needs or challenging behaviour. However, this is often unsuccessful because of the frequently different expectations and needs of refugee children and the citizen children. One girl in this situation was frustrated that the teacher "didn't help much and shouted a lot" and her English was slow to improve. One teacher felt this was an intimidating situation for refugee children and another went as far as to say this approach could be "creating trauma of a different sort" for young refugees. A number of young people confirmed they had found this situation difficult:

"The students kept shouting and not listening to the teacher, so the teacher doesn't teach, so you miss a lot and you don't get to ask questions."

As a result of this need to cope with new needs with few extra resources, one teacher spoke of the school being at "bursting point", explaining that they "already have a big workload, are rushed off their feet, frustrated, and can't plan".

Nonetheless, all the professionals we spoke to reported that the response of asylum-seeking children to education was in general very positive, and the comments of the young people themselves supported this. One boy described how hard work had paid off:

"At the beginning when I was in the class, the teacher was talking about something I didn't know. I was just laughing, you know, telling myself I wish I [was] understanding. But then I really tried hard and hard and work and used to watch TV and get to know things like that."

A teacher suggested that it would be encouraging if there were more recognition of achievement by separated refugee children in schools because often their results may not be at the top of the range in absolute terms, but their achievements are great in relation to their starting point.

Good practice

In one local authority we looked at, Quality Protects funding has been used to appoint an education support officer to designate teachers to monitor and promote the educational interests of "looked after" children in their school.

There also is a support teacher employed to identify the educational needs of refugee children living in a residential home and find them a place in school. She also spends time giving in-class support to those who need it and, whenever possible, homework support. The teacher liaises with home managers, link workers, social workers and teachers to develop a personal education plan for each child.

A great deal of emphasis was placed on the value of this support teacher by all four young people we spoke to who had lived in the home. Many other young people expressed a wish to have someone in this kind of role where they lived or went to school or college. One young person living in a residential home said:

"I am studying difficult subjects like geography and IT [information technology] and the support workers here can't help me because the subjects are too hard. I need more expert help, like a tutor."

Even where young people had the benefit of a support teacher visiting their residential home (see box above), the young people there still felt they needed more support with their homework.

Good practice

Social services in one area have linked up with a local university for a Millennium Volunteers Project, in which students volunteer as educational mentors for young people in residential homes offering homework support, and organise leisure and sporting activities with them.

THE ETHNIC MINORITY AND TRAVELLER ACHIEVEMENT GRANT (EMTAG)

There is clearly a need for schools to develop a broader range of ways to cope with the educational needs of young separated refugees. To some extent this is being developed through the Ethnic Minority and Traveller Achievement Grant (EMTAG). The way in which the EMTAG is used to provide a service varies from place to place but essentially it does three things for students who are Travellers or from minority ethnic communities, including refugees:

- provides staff to give additional language support to students for whom English is not their first language

- advises and supports teachers not used to working with Travellers and students from minority ethnic communities. This includes in-service training for teachers

- where possible, provides an educational assessment of students in their first language.

Forty per cent of funds are currently committed to London and Kent.[41] Responsibility for at least 75 per cent of the grant (or the amount over a £150,000 threshold) is devolved directly to schools.[42] Schools can then use the money to buy services from the local education authority (LEA) or elsewhere. This has resulted in some LEAs developing a flexible floating support service to provide a pool of expertise and resources that schools can make use of, as and when they need them in order to respond to an influx of refugee children. In the one region where we asked education professionals about the devolution of EMTAG funds to schools, they felt strongly that it limited schools' capacity to meet the complex support needs of newly arriving refugee pupils because of bureaucratic procedures and the time lapse between applying for and receiving funds.[43]

Good practice

In a number of areas the EMTAG team has achieved a degree of flexibility through the development of a fast-response team of English language teachers to cope with the continually changing demand in schools during the year. The EMTAG teachers provide short introductory courses in "survival English" and in-class support.

All the students we spoke to were impressed with the support they had received from EMTAG teachers:

"There's [an] English support room where they're really helping you. It's really useful because whenever you feel sorry or sad that you can't speak English... I would just go straight over... and... [the teacher] was there hugging you and holding you to give you the feeling – to make you feel good."

---

[41] Children's Consortium, *Briefing on education and refugee children*, 2000.

[42] Children's Consortium, *Briefing on education and refugee children*, 2000.

[43] Ibid.

There seems to be an imbalance in the amount of EMTAG support available in different areas. For example, one area with 22 young separated refugees and relatively few children from a minority ethnic group had nine full-time EMTAG teaching posts. Another area with 55 young separated refugees and over 300 young asylum-seekers had only 4.6 posts. The system in this area "survives by simply not going out to some of the schools that need them". This imbalance may be explained by the fact that LEAs must contribute match EMTAG funding at 42 per cent of the central government grant, or else by the fact that it can take some time for LEAs to gear up to meeting the needs of new refugee arrivals.

In a survey of 58 LEAs published in September 2001,[44] although authorities and their schools reported that they were "willing to rise to the challenge of meeting the needs of the new arrivals", 90 per cent of authorities saw their EMTAG budgets as insufficient to achieve this.

In July 2000, the Department for Education and Employment (now the Department for Employment and Skills) announced a one-year ring-fenced grant worth up to £500 per student for schools supporting NASS-registered asylum-seeking children in specific areas designated by NASS. The grant will be available for the academic year 2001/2002 under the same terms as last year.

One EMTAG co-ordinator described the grant as "a knee-jerk response" to the massive challenge facing schools in dispersal areas. Nonetheless, the grant was welcomed by many teachers and other education professionals and has been used to provide additional language support using bi-lingual staff, school uniforms and travel warrants for transport to school. In the cases we looked at, the grant had been secured quickly and made available as soon as the young people started school, but the amount was considered by teachers to be far too small, as it covers only the first few weeks in school. Moreover, the support package is the "property" of the school, so if the young person moves school (which is not unlikely) they cannot take the support with them.

The school can claim the grant only on production of a NASS identification number. Therefore, young separated refugees who are not supported by NASS (which includes all unaccompanied children) are not eligible for the extra support. The assumption is that all unaccompanied refugees are attending schools that are already well equipped to work with refugee students, but we found that this was not necessarily the case. For example, in one area which was not a NASS cluster area, there were almost 100 unaccompanied minors, and the overwhelming concern of the young people themselves and of the professionals was that they were not receiving adequate education.

---

[44] Mott, 2001.

IN COLLEGE

ESOL programmes in colleges were generally highly regarded. Even a boy attending a college unaccustomed to working with refugees said:

"There are a lot of people there who are really nice and help, and that's good."

He is taking four A levels and an English language course. He said:

"We have all the support we need. Like, for example, in computing and maths, physics you have one day… where you can go up there and ask something if you want to know."

One education professional said that many pupils do not recognise their need for additional English language education and have unrealistic expectations:

"The problem is they come with a dream, maybe that their parents told them when they left, like be a doctor or an engineer. It is a dream they hold on to. It is hard enough for anyone to fulfil those dreams, but it is three or four years before they have the level of English language [needed] for university."

A number of colleges, especially in London, have developed ways of helping young refugees set realistic goals and achieve them.

Good practice

At one London college there are approximately 500 students on ESOL courses, of whom the majority are refugees. Young separated refugees are enrolled on full-time and part-time ESOL courses, as well as mainstream/ESOL link-up courses and mainstream courses. All full-time courses include two hours of information technology, and the higher-level classes include tasters in mainstream subjects. The courses are split by age so that all "Young Learners" are in class together.

In two London colleges we looked at, tutors work with pupils on an action plan to set realistic objectives and select courses where they are most likely to make progress. Connexions advisers (see Chapter 3, The policy context) have a remit to work on this kind of action plan, in order to maximise the educational opportunities of young people, including refugees, to get them into training and work experience. The service will specifically target the most excluded young people.

5.7.3 Pastoral support

Adults and young people alike viewed education as not only an arena for learning but also a route to integration, as well as a means of alleviating boredom and of structuring their lives. Similarly, education has been recognised as the one area in which refugee children can gain a degree of constancy and have contact with non-refugee children.[45] Participation in full-time education also ensures some degree of adult contact. As one youth worker put it, without education they have little to do and can appear threatening, standing around the streets in groups:

> *"They are a population of young men who are denied a legitimate income and denied meaningful daytime activity, they are outside of parental and family guidance, it is a problem waiting to happen… They look menacing in the centre of town in groups but they are not, they are desperately bored."*

Inevitably, there is a need for pastoral support in school or college for young people who are separated from their parents. Our research identified teachers and education support workers as a key source of care for young separated refugees who are in education. A number of students explained how, in their eyes, a teacher had taken on the role of surrogate parent:

> *"My dad's not here, my mum's not here, but actually… I can say clearly that* [teacher] *is like my dad here in this country."*

However, there are very few teachers, or even education support workers, who feel able to adequately fulfil this need because of a lack of time or support from their management:

> *"They need a bit of mothering that nobody else seems to be doing and I think that some of the unaccompanied feel that they can turn to us, that we'll listen to them and try to help them. I think what we get* [from our management] *is 'oh well, that's not really your job'."* (Education support worker)

EMTAG does not have funds to allow teachers to spend time on pastoral care and this role should fall to specialist support staff such as Connexions personal advisers. However, this was not happening in many areas and EMTAG staff were offering support beyond normal professional boundaries, such as using their own money to support children:

> *"If we had not given the money from our pockets the children would have missed about ten or twelve weeks of schooling."* (EMTAG staff)

---

[45] Rutter, 1998.

HARASSMENT AND BULLYING

The integration of some young refugees into the school environment is hampered by harassment and bullying, which in turn means they are not learning as much English from their peers, adding to their isolation. Although it is sometimes difficult to be certain about the reasons for harassment, from our interviews it was clear that many experiences of harassment were due to racism and xenophobia.

Harassment appeared to be more common in schools than in colleges. A total of 36 young people reported direct and indirect experience of harassment, racism or bullying, some of which they linked to their status as an asylum-seeker or refugee:

> *"They* [English boys] *say, 'Why did you come from Kosovo* [to] *England? Why do* [you come to] *my school? Why you not go in different school?' Sometimes they have fights and ... the English boys they smack them first and then they go straight away home, and to the police and say we smack them first. We have to go after* [to the police station] *to give interview about we not do nothing... I* [was] *a little bit upset about the boys* [who lied]."

> *"At first people would swear at me and I didn't know why, they would say 'f***ing Kosovan'... It makes feel bad, maybe they have problem with someone else."*

Some of the harassment came from other refugees. An interpreter described a serious attack on a boy by a group of young refugees from another country:

> *"They scare him... two times they have beaten him up... four days ago he was beaten up behind the school... That night they beat him they said they were going to kill him. All his clothes were taken so now he's got nothing."*

Good practice

A youth worker for a voluntary organisation has been asked by some schools to help them address the bullying of refugee children. She holds weekly sessions aimed at encouraging discussion about bullying issues and providing support.

Behaviour support services, education psychology services and youth services are available to schools for tackling bullying, and every school has an anti-bullying strategy. However, greatest emphasis was placed, by professionals and young people alike, on the role of teachers in encouraging the integration of refugee children in school, although current techniques to deal with the issue clearly have limited effectiveness. One boy described how a teacher can at least stop students from making remarks about refugees:

"Only a few incidents happen, but not a lot. Half of them made remarks about being refugees, when the teacher found out they had a serious talk with them, some are hesitant now but it didn't stop their feelings… It is difficult to get on with the other boys, they have their own jokes."

Education professionals generally felt that teachers should address racism and discrimination directly. One professional felt that secondary school teachers were more likely to ignore incidents because of the pressure to get through the curriculum, and a lack of time for pastoral work. She felt this left children feeling vulnerable. (Racism is dealt with in greater detail in section 5.8, Social networks.)

5.7.4 Financial issues

There are significant costs involved in attending school or college which are not always adequately covered by the existing systems for supporting young separated refugees.

The Immigration and Asylum Act (1999) specifically amended previous legislation to ensure that all asylum-seeking and refugee children are entitled to free school meals. However, the systems for claiming this entitlement are extremely bureaucratic in many areas and there is considerable misinformation on the subject. For example, in one area social services were paying for young refugees' school meals and then claiming the money back through the Education Department.

Social services can use their discretion to decide whether or not they provide funds for school uniforms.[46] At least half of the social services departments we looked at did not have a systematic approach to providing school uniforms. On other issues where social services exercise discretion (such as other clothing allowances) there was frequently a lack of information available as to how decisions were made and a lack of understanding about the policy.

College tuition fees for all refugee pupils are paid by colleges. The majority of young refugees are not eligible for the Access grants that cover all other associated expenses because, to be eligible, a young person must have leave to remain *and* have been in the country for more than three years.

The Student Support Service in one college we looked at manages a discretionary, private fund of over £20,000, which can be used to cover students' college-related expenses, such as books and materials. Two months into the academic year 2000/2001, the fund was already £5,000 overspent. Some £8,000 of the fund expenditure was on ESOL students, most of whom were refugees.

---

[46] Asylum-seeking children are not entitled to standard school uniform grant through the LEA.

Those asylum-seekers whose relatives receive vouchers in lieu of cash find their situation particularly difficult. They are unable to use vouchers to pay for travel expenses to college, and the college canteen does not accept vouchers. As a result, one member of staff reported, "We know there are students who don't eat all day."

5.8 Social networks

Main findings

- Young separated refugees are not guaranteed adequate and appropriate support just because they are accompanied by a relation. Many derive the most support from their refugee peers.

- Many young separated refugees are socially excluded as a result of poverty, discrimination and lack of participation in full-time or mainstream education.

- Racism is a problem in all areas we looked at and exists between the citizen and refugee populations and within the refugee population.

Key factors affecting young people's access to social networks:
- Do they have family or members of their community origin living nearby?
- Are they in education?
- Do they receive adequate financial support?

5.8.1 Family support

UNACCOMPANIED REFUGEES

In our research with young separated refugees we did not seek to find out how the young people had become separated from their parents, nor did we seek to explore the level of contact they had with their family. The decision was made because this can be an especially emotional subject and researchers did not want to open up emotions that we were not in a position to deal with adequately.

Nonetheless, a number of young people volunteered information and described their separation from their parents as a source of anxiety and distress. This distress was compounded in some cases by their awareness that they have no automatic right to family reunification in UK law, despite the Human Rights Act (1998) and UNCRC (see 5.9, Immigration issues).

ACCOMPANIED REFUGEES

Many professionals we spoke to had concerns over the vulnerability of young refugees who are the responsibility of siblings or other relatives who would not ordinarily be responsible for their care. In particular, a number of adults had specific concerns in relation to young girls. The example below illustrates the kind of problem that can face a young person living in the care of people who are not their usual carers.

> One young girl arrived here with her older sibling and they later argued. She moved to live with another sibling with whom she also fell out because they wanted her to marry an older English businessman. She did not want to do this, but was trapped because her siblings claimed her child benefit and had her identity and immigration papers. Without papers, the girl could not get access to benefits or support from the asylum team. The student support service at her college advocated on her behalf and eventually the asylum team agreed to support her.

However, where a family member acts as a guardian to younger siblings or other relatives there are clearly benefits in some – particularly emotional – respects. It was clear that having some relatives in the UK was regarded as an advantage by the young people we interviewed. One boy described how relatives had helped him:

"I found family members. I thought were dead, they help me, they buy me clothes and helped make my home nice."

Another young person who lived with her older brother and sister appeared to be getting a lot of support from them. They had helped her register with a doctor, dentist and solicitor and to get access to education. In these situations the guardian, rather than an allocated social worker, may become the key advocate for the family. But – especially when that guardian is young and where there is no monitoring from social services – the negatives can far outweigh the positives. Unfortunately, perhaps for reasons of mistrust of authority or unawareness of entitlements, these young guardians are unlikely to be effective in the role, as the following case demonstrates.

One young person, on reaching the age of 18, became legal guardian to his two younger brothers. The family had seen a social worker when they first arrived over two years earlier, but not since. The oldest brother was finding it difficult to act as family advocate as he was largely unaware of his family's entitlements. This was compounded by his scepticism about the merits of seeking advice and help:

> *"Since living here I have learned not to trust anyone… We have had to learn not to rely on other people."*

This approach meant the carer had to take on a great deal of responsibility. He talked in particular about the financial pressure:

> *"It is a great pressure on me having to care for my brothers. I am having to give up my college course so I can support them. We don't have enough money to survive. Since moving to [this area], I have been put on this stupid voucher system. I hate it. It is so humiliating. I see it as a form of racism."*

Within this context the material well-being of the family declined considerably. Having lost all their benefits due to bad advice, they struggled to survive on the oldest sibling's part-time wage. Heating in their home was confined to one room. The youngest member had to walk a long way to school because he did not realise that he was entitled to a bus pass and he had been told he was no longer entitled to free school meals.

5.8.2 Community support

The young people we interviewed tended to socialise with and support each other through informal friendship groups, rather than through more formal community organisations. Such organisations do exist, particularly among the more established ethnic groups, but few of the young people we spoke to showed an interest in finding out more about them.

However, where young people were in contact with community organisations, they found them very helpful. For example, one young person had been helped to register with a doctor with the assistance of an adult asylum-seeker of the same nationality. This practical support can compensate for where social services are not able to provide it. Community support can also bring emotional advantages, as one boy described:

> *"We meet at the community centre at least once a month to have a social gathering and we can talk about some of our problems. All of us are missing our culture and our country."*

Case study: Salam

Salam is isolated from her community and intimidated by her environment. Her story also illustrates the instability and anxiety that can be caused when an individual's needs are not fully taken into account when making care arrangements, and emphasises the need to include a consideration of the location of the placement as part of that assessment.

Salam presented herself to social services in a city in the Midlands in the summer of 2000. She was alone and 16 years old. She is a practising Muslim.

Social services placed her in a shared house with a woman and three men. Neither her bedroom nor the bathroom had a lock on the door. She asked social services three or four times for a lock. She said that she cried every time she went to them and she "suffered very much" living in that house. While she was living in the house she was attending college but she was followed everywhere by two or three refugee men. This made her afraid and she stopped going to college. She sat in her accommodation all day.

She was moved from the shared house after six weeks. Since then she has lived in three hostels and she was expecting to move again at any time. The hostel where she was living at the time of the interview was in poor condition – the kitchen was unusable, the toilet was broken and there was no light and the hostel had "a very bad smell".

All the moves make her anxious that the Home Office will not be able to get in touch with her:

> "Because every time they are changing me, the Home Office letter cannot come to me. Every week they say I will move."

She would like to move to London to be near people from her country of origin and her solicitor and to get more support. She was suffering from the strain of her isolated existence:

> "England is a very nice country… Social services is good in some places but my experience is not good. I can't sleep and I can't eat… I get headaches because I am thinking too much and I not feel happy."

5.8.3 Peer support

SUPPORT FROM CITIZEN PEERS

> "My biggest need is to have more contact with English people." (Boy, aged 17)

School or college tends to be the focal point for young refugees to meet and interact with citizen peers. The young separated refugees we spoke to had varying experiences of this but most had found it difficult at first.

A 15-year-old boy described a typical story of being the new boy:

"When I was [at] school the other boys were joking about something. When people are new coming to school, you know kids, the other boys were acting differently. Then I start thinking how am I getting away from this. Then I bought a football and then I was kicking with myself and some of them came over and said, 'Friend, can I play with you?', 'Yeah, sure, go on', and after all of them came. Then when I was going to lunchtime all of them were waiting outside for me, to play football, and that's the way I found many friends."

One boy, who had been in the UK for over seven years, said he was no longer interested in spending time with people from his country of origin:

"I have so many friends here. Since I came here I hear nothing about [country of origin], *I heard they got a new president or something. I can't be bothered with them* [people from country of origin] *because they always talk about politics."*

Yet others continued to have difficulties integrating even after a considerable time in the UK. For example, one girl from Africa who had been here for over two years described feelings of intimidation about mixing with English people in college:

"The English people talk to themselves and we sit separately. We are different. I don't smile. I don't talk to them because I want to keep my dignity. If I am close to them they will underestimate me, I will feel a failure, I don't speak their language properly. I have a friend who is white, but I want to be distant and I don't want to let her know everything about me for some reason, I am scared of people."

The experiences described by these young people illustrate the potential conflict between their identities as refugees and their identities as young people with feelings and experiences like those of many citizen young people. Each individual must find a way to cope with this. A number of professionals we spoke to believed that some dropped their religion or cultural practices in an attempt to fit in with citizen children and submerge their refugee identity. A support teacher felt this happened as a result of anti-refugee feelings in schools:

"Almost all of them don't want to talk about being refugees in school, because of the stigma; yet… in schools there is a policy of multiculture, respect everybody's background. But where refugees are concerned they have got the sense very clearly that they should keep quiet about it. So they will say they are from Saudi Arabia and they will talk about their

parents having done something as though their parents are living here, so they are trying to cover up all the time."

Others, however, were very conscious of the need to retain their cultural identity. One boy said:

"I am frightened I lose my culture, my language and my religion. I have no Koran in my house and do not understand everything at mosque."

To counteract this, one social worker recommended activities that could make them feel proud of their heritage and bolster their self-esteem.

Most of the young people we spoke to did not have many citizen friends, partly because of their limited opportunities to meet them – especially if they were enrolled in an ESOL rather than a mainstream class – but not because of a lack of interest on the part of young refugees. Many of them felt that it was beneficial to have citizen friends, although the language barrier can limit this possibility. One boy said English people sometimes spoke to him, but he could not understand what they were saying – in terms of both language and culture. This situation worried him because he was afraid they would think he did not like English people, which was not true. So instead he spent his time with people from his own country. However, one young person we spoke to put his lack of English friends down to racism:

"People here are racists, they don't talk to you. I don't have any English friends here."

Generally, though, most young refugees and professionals believed that a lack of English language ability, access to school and a lack of money were the reasons why young separated refugees had few opportunities to meet adults or young people outside the refugee community.

A suitable and supportive placement is likely to encourage young refugees to make friends. For example, two boys placed with English foster carers demonstrated that they had fully integrated into local life and appeared to be confident and happy.

SUPPORT FROM REFUGEE PEERS

The young people placed great value on their friendships, which were usually with people from their own country of origin. One 13-year-old girl described the importance of friendship:

"The advice I'd give to other people like me coming here is to find people to talk to. Close friends with whom you can share your problems and help you. It is very hard living like this and you get upset and sad, you can't cope without them."

The opportunities for girls to make friends are even more limited than they are for boys, as there are comparatively fewer separated refugee girls. One young girl felt very sharply the contrast between her social life here and in her country of origin, even though she had been in the UK for almost two years. Young refugee girls may be made more vulnerable to exploitation as a result of weak peer support, as the following case shows.

One young unaccompanied girl told support workers she had met a new English boyfriend who had come to her hostel to visit people. She told the workers how kind he was and how he bought her food and clothes. The workers were suspicious of his intentions and put the girl in touch with a support group called "Alone in London", who supported the young girl. According to the support workers, the girl now believes she had a lucky escape from a potentially exploitative relationship.

In situations where peer support is lacking there can be serious consequences in terms of social isolation. This can lead young people to devise their own way of linking up with community members.

Two 16-year-old boys felt isolated by the lack of peer support they received where they were living. They said:

"We hate it here, there is no one we can relate to, there are only a few of us and no one else who is our age."

They devised a strategy to escape their isolation by trying to join people they knew in another part of the country, which involved not eating in order to save money to travel:

"I wanted to leave [city] and I have tried. I once spent several weeks not eating so I could save enough money. I travelled to [city in the Midlands] with the money."

On reaching their destination they attempted to register with social services, but found that their support could not be transferred. They were sent back to Yorkshire and Humberside.

Good practice

In one city a local voluntary organisation, in conjunction with social services, runs an activity group for young unaccompanied refugees. Once a week they might go ice-skating, play pool, go swimming or make a meal together. Gatherings are arranged through flyers distributed by social services when the young people collect their weekly allowance.

The group is particularly aimed at new arrivals who are just finding their feet, as it gives them a chance to meet other people in a similar position, and to talk to the adult volunteers for advice or support if they wish.

The group used to get about £10 a week from social services to cover their costs, but recently they have requested a little more. Save the Children has recently made a grant of approximately £800 to the group to cover the costs of some activities this year.

5.8.4 Social activities and barriers

"It's not a very good life, we don't know where to go or what to do – nothing." (Boy, aged 16)

The limited opportunities that young separated refugees have for social activities were encapsulated by one boy who, when asked what he did in his free time, said:

"I have five options: BBC1, BBC2, ITV, Channel 4 and Channel 5."

Others listed their activities as: homework, watching television, reading, going for walks, playing football, visiting friends and going to the mosque or church. Among the activities they mentioned that they would like to do, or do more of, were football, computing, homework tuition, visiting friends, swimming, going to the gym, aerobics and martial arts.

Some of the colleges organise occasional trips for their students. These were very popular, and many students said they would like to see more of the area where they live. Any excursion at all provides welcome relief for these young people, whose lives are characterised by almost uninterrupted monotony. Other boys suggested that being busy helped to distract them from deeper troubles, highlighting the danger inherent in inactivity:

"I sit in my room, then I go to college and I go nowhere else, I don't know anywhere outside my route to college and back."

"I am trying to make myself as busy as I can because I will never think about my past or what's happened to me."

One boy was clearly frustrated by not being able to work and use his time constructively:

"I feel we are being kept here like pigs with nothing to do all day. We want to be able to work, spend our time productively."

Asylum-seekers are not permitted to seek work, or even to do voluntary work, until they have been in the country for over six months and even then they are likely to find it difficult to enter the job market. The Home Office grants permission to work only to the head of the family, so if a young person is accompanied by an adult they must apply in their own right and may not receive permssion to work at all.

> **Good practice**
> One London scheme attempts to alleviate the boredom of the everyday experience of being a refugee, and to help separated children integrate into local life. The children are taken away on holiday at the beginning of the summer, and then through the summer it runs a group through which it introduces them to local services and sports so that they integrate more with citizen children.

A sense of social exclusion, the wait for an asylum decision (see 5.9, Immigration issues) and poverty seemed to generate the boredom described by many young people. More specifically it seemed to be generated by less-than-full-time participation in education and a sense that they had lesser rights than those of citizen children, as illustrated by one accompanied boy when talking about his accommodation.

> The boy lived in a block of flats where the neighbours played loud music through the night and he could not sleep. He came to college feeling tired. He had not complained because he felt that, as a refugee, he had no right to:
>
> *"We are refugees and we have no rights. We don't want trouble, so we don't complain... the British people in the other flats don't say anything and they have power."*

One young refugee felt that refugees exist in an underclass of their own in this country, and that even if some people in the local community responded well to refugees, others, such as decision-makers, did not:

"There are different lives in one country. There are people with low incomes but they are not like us, the refugees. Even if local people are OK, the officials do not react well. They think we are taking their money because they pay tax."

A number of professionals agreed that there was institutionalised discrimination against young separated refugees. A social worker said:

"They are treated worse than indigenous children."

This is exacerbated by the fact that refugee children are unlikely to ask for their full entitlements because they do not know what their entitlements are. And so the vicious circle continues and entrenches their poverty and social exclusion. Young people described how their poverty had directly made them feel excluded:

"I would like to go to the cinema, but I have to save money for more important things — like things for school and clothes. My friends tell me the plot and then I pretend I know, that I have been to the films. One more thing that pushes us aside is not having proper clothes. All the other young people have designer clothes, people don't want to play or make friends with you if you are not wearing the right things."

Most of the young people we spoke to said they could not do the things they would like to due to lack of money and for those living on vouchers the situation is particularly difficult. One boy was worried that his source of social activity was about to be cut off because he could not afford the fees to play football. He said:

"These kind of barriers remind you that you are different."

Some local authorities have attempted to make leisure facilities more accessible to young refugees. For example, in one area a number of leisure centres have been made available to refugees on specific days and this has proved popular. However, not all those interviewed felt able to participate. There was inadequate information about the facility and several young people interviewed had not known that the service was available. Others had experienced inter-ethnic tensions there, and so, being anxious to avoid trouble, stayed away. Others simply did not enjoy sports. In another area cards are given to young separated refugees to enable them to use certain leisure facilities without charge.

CRIME

Naturally, people devise strategies in an effort to cope with their poverty and a number of professionals speculated that young separated refugees might turn to crime. However, members of the youth offending team in one area said that young separated refugees' contact with the youth justice system had been "surprisingly low". Those separated refugees who are known to youth offending teams rarely fit comfortably into existing projects, partly because they tend to have limited English language ability. Those cases which had come to their attention related to shoplifting, street violence and motoring-related offences (though not car theft), which the team's members believed was predictable:

> *"The shoplifting because of their reduced income and all the goodies of Western civilisation around them; violence because of the prejudice they face, and cars because of their lack of understanding about the rules."*

Youth offending teams have a preventive remit to support interventions with high-risk groups.

In one region, however, where young separated refugees' access to education and social activities are especially limited, 3 out of the 18 young people we interviewed had been charged with an offence. The charges against all three were later dropped. A fourth was arrested in error as described below.

After trying to help a friend who was suffering multiple injuries after being attacked, one boy was arrested. His problems began because, being unable to speak English, he could not explain to the police the motives behind his intervention. The police decided to hold him overnight at the station until an interpreter could be found and his story explained and verified.

5.8.5 Harassment and racism

REFUGEES AND THE CITIZEN POPULATION

Generally, the situation in areas without a large minority ethnic community was found to be worse in terms of harassment and racism than in areas that are relatively multicultural. In London less than a quarter of the young people interviewed said they had experienced bullying or harassment. By contrast, in a region in the north of England almost half (8 out of 18) of the young people reported instances of racially motivated physical and/or verbal abuse.

In one area without a large minority ethnic community, young people reported a high level of serious attacks such as the following page.

> A 17-year-old boy from Kosovo described a terrifying experience of violence on his doorstep:
>
> *"I went to the house with my mates, we were eating some food. Someone knocked on the door and he asked me for bus money. I asked my mates and they had none, he started swearing and forcing the door. I told him go away now. They start swearing again. I was pushing him outside. He took my shirt and broke it. Someone behind took a brick and threw it at my head... Twenty-five or 26-year-old hit me with a brick again. We went to community worker's house and then afterwards to hospital."*

And yet there were also reports of overt racial abuse and assault from white people in more ethnically mixed areas. For example, a group of black female students described being the victims of such abuse:

> *"We were going to get on* [the bus] *and this man started hitting me so hard. I was so scared. He says, 'Get back you little black cow' or something. I was really scared and then these boys went past and they started laughing and shouting, 'Black, black, black.' They were all white – the boys and the man."*

This kind of experience should serve as a reminder that it is misleading to divide Britain into "white" areas where refugees will automatically face racism and hostility, and multi-ethnic areas where they will not. The reality is more complex. Multi-ethnic areas tend also to be socially disadvantaged areas where conflicts may break out, and where "strangers" such as young refugees may be perceived as particular targets. We must also look at the social and economic situation in the area rather than simply at the ethnic mix.

For example, in one northern city the majority of asylum-seekers in the city are housed in some of the most deprived areas, well known for their social problems and, according to one education professional, young people living there are vulnerable to attack:

> *"People who are responsible for housing are sometimes placing* [young asylum-seekers] *where there is an acute tendency of racism... they're isolated and they go home after school, they don't want to come out because there is a tendency that children might hit them, they might racially abuse them, all sorts of things."*

One boy was so afraid that he felt seriously threatened. He said:

> *"I came here to save my life not lose it".*

Furthermore, it should be noted that young black refugees also experienced hostility from other black people, as one student reported:

"I think it's sometimes because of colour. Some of them say 'Oh, look at the Pakis' because they use words like that – why can't they just say Pakistani? Last time someone called me black African – trying to insult me – I said I'm happy to be black, I'm proud to be black and African! Even some Africans say it! I don't understand why."

This reinforces the recognition that non-white minorities are not homogeneous, and it is mistaken therefore to believe that refugees can simply be placed in multi-ethnic areas where a perceived common affinity will somehow lead to their needs being met.

Some of these experiences are clearly examples of racist abuse. Others might be interpreted as examples of bullying in and around school and as street crime without a specifically racist motive. However, the students experienced these in racist terms, not least because racist insults often accompanied the attacks on them.

In some areas there were very few reports of racism from the young people. However, we should not take this as meaning racism did not occur in these areas. One reason for this may be that some young refugees are not "visible" to the citizen community. In one area, none of those who had not experienced harassment was attending a school and none apparently felt able to make use of any local community and leisure facilities. So although they might not have been experiencing harassment this could have been because they were not exposing themselves to situations in which harassment might happen, and as a result were not able to enjoy local amenities either.

BETWEEN REFUGEES

Racism towards young separated refugees is not initiated solely from within the citizen community. Racism between refugee groups is also common. Very often the basis for antagonisms within the refugee community is rooted in non-racial, non-national and non-ethnic as well as inter-racial, inter-national and inter-ethnic factors.

In one house a Kurdish young refugee was living with other Kurds from a different area who spoke a different dialect. While he was accommodated with people from the same ethnic group, the isolation he was feeling in this country was heightened when his accent, dialect and the village where he was from became the subject of the others' jokes:

"I want to change this house... they are bigger than me. They boss me about... they speak a different dialect and make jokes about the town and area I come from."

A number of adults we spoke to said they had come across evidence of both racism and sexism among some young refugees. This was disputed by other adults, yet it raises questions about the ease of integration of young refugees into local culture. Statements by young people themselves suggest that, given the opportunity to tackle their prejudices head on, young separated refugees can integrate successfully. For example, one boy described how he was alarmed to find he would be living with two young black refugees, and yet within a couple of months he was firm friends with the boys and had dismissed his ill-founded reservations:

> *"I didn't like black people* [when I arrived] *because we haven't got black people in Kosovo. But now it's OK because I live with them, sleep with them, eat with them. I am very good friends with them."*

5.9 Immigration issues

"I lost my parents, they have been killed… I am happy to be here, my life was dangerous."
(Boy, aged 14)

"You have to wait for everything, I will be dead waiting." (Boy, aged 17)

Main findings

- **Young separated refugees suffer considerable anxiety as a result of substantial delays in the wait for an asylum decision. This is compounded by a lack of information from both legal representatives and the Home Office.**

- **There is some evidence of inconsistent decision-making by the Home Office on asylum applications.**

Key factors in determining a young person's experience of the asylum process:
- How long do they have to wait for a final asylum decision?
- What is the quality of their legal representation?
- Does the Home Office makes any mistakes when processing their claim?

5.9.1 Legal representatives

Most of the young people we spoke to without asylum decisions felt unable to judge whether or not their legal representative was doing a good job on their behalf, although a small number felt their representative was not committed to their case. One boy said:

"My solicitor doesn't care about me, nobody cares about us."

The newly created Immigration Services Commissioner[47] will be responsible for operating procedures and regulations, introduced in October 2000, on who can provide immigration advice or services. It is hoped that they will provide a safeguard against sub-standard legal advice being given to asylum-seekers. However, there will still be no way of judging whether a legal representative has the specific skills required to work with children and young people.[48]

There seems to be widespread confusion about all matters relating to the legal process, and this is rooted in a lack of accessible information. Many of the young

---

[47] The scheme was introduced by the Immigration and Asylum Act (1999).

[48] See also Ayotte, 1998.

separated refugees we spoke to felt that the information and advice they had received was poor or seemed hurried, and left them in a state of confusion.

All the areas we looked at outside of London reported a shortage of immigration law specialists; a number of young people interviewed in each of these areas had a legal representative in London and had to travel there to see them, or else had to communicate with them by telephone. Travel can be expensive and young people were not always clear that this cost should be covered by social services or their legal representative. Telephone conversations can prove difficult if the young person's English language ability is limited.

In addition, again largely in areas outside of London, there is a scarcity of interpreters available to work with legal representatives and ensure that the young person understands the questions being asked, provides all the necessary information and has their own questions answered. Clearly, this is crucial to the outcome of the asylum application itself.

A number of young people and professionals reported that considerable difficulties had arisen where the client and young person spoke different dialects or used different colloquialisms. For instance, in Sudan the word "balish" means "stop" but in Syria, Lebanon, Jordan and Palestine "balish" means "started". If a young person uses this word to describe a war, for example, this kind of difference in meaning could seriously affect their case.

Young people are mostly referred to legal representatives through social services or sometimes through friends. Others, though, met their representatives in a somewhat unconventional manner, which might provide opportunities for the unscrupulous. One boy met his representative at a bus station:

> *"When I first came here I was in Victoria Station and I met a guy, he was an interpreter for the solicitor and he took me to the immigration office of the solicitor."*

Those social services who were familiar with the Refugee Council's Panel of Advisers sometimes passed young people on to them for onward referral to a legal representative. The Panel Adviser will also accompany the child to any immigration interviews and guide them through the asylum process. One boy we spoke to who had been in contact with a Panel Adviser had found their help invaluable after the Home Office lost his papers.

5.9.2 Asylum screening interviews

Young people who do not apply for asylum at the port of entry ("in-country" applicants) must attend an asylum screening interview at the Home Office in Croydon (although unaccompanied children are not usually interviewed about their case). One adult who accompanies young people to screening interviews described it as a very intimidating experience:

> *"The whole thing is designed to make you feel like scum, no concessions, from the minute you walk in the door it's 'what are you here for?' – that's how it starts and it gets no better."*

This is despite the fact that the 1993 immigration rules state that all interviews should be conducted in a child-sensitive manner.[49] It clearly requires emotional preparation for the child to make this visit. One young person waited six hours at the office, only to be told that his papers had been lost and he needed to return the following week. Three weeks later the papers were found and emotions were raised again for the next visit.

All unaccompanied minors should be accompanied to this interview by an adult.[50] There are certain legal rights and procedures that the accompanying adult must be aware of if they are to successfully support the child through this crucial stage of the asylum process. For example, it was reported by young people in one area that they had been given adult asylum application forms to complete, which come with a 14-day time limit for completion and submission. Unaccompanied minors have been refused asylum on non-compliance grounds because they have failed to meet this requirement.[51] This strongly suggests there is a need to monitor the level of young people being refused asylum on non-compliance grounds. According to one Panel Adviser, in situations like this an appeal against the refusal is likely to be successful, but it creates unnecessary anxiety for the young person in the meantime.

The frequency of these kinds of administrative mistakes by the Home Office highlights the need for young separated refugees to be accompanied to screening interviews and for that accompanying adult to be well informed about processes and legal procedures and able to explain them to the young person. Many of the young people we interviewed had not been accompanied to their screening interview and on at least one occasion the accompanying adult had not been allowed to enter the interview room with the young person. On another occasion, a social worker accompanied two boys to their interview, where they were detained on suspicion of being over 18 years, but the social worker had felt powerless to intervene.

The need for better advice on asylum procedures is made clear by the following examples. One boy claimed that at his interview he was told no decision would be made until he was an adult; this was clearly a mistake but it is not clear exactly what the immigration officer had said or intended him to understand:

---

[49] 1993 Immigration Rules, HC395, paras 349–52.

[50] Ibid.

[51] See Younge, 2001.

"I went for an interview in Croydon and they told me come back when I am over 18 and my case will be dealt with then. While I am a minor they are not going to do anything."

A boy, aged 18, attended his screening interview and was told to return in two weeks to get his identification. When he returned he was told the identification had been lost, and he should come back again in another two weeks. This pattern was repeated a total of five times over a period of nearly three months.

Each time he went to Croydon he had to miss college and buy a ticket to get there. He saw a different person every time and had to queue for between three and four hours. He said the staff were very rude to him.

On his most recent visit, he told staff he had diabetes and he was given a number in order that he could register with a doctor, but still did not receive his identification. He consulted a community organisation which told him he couldn't get a solicitor without identification papers, so he must keep going back every fortnight until he got them.

5.9.3 Asylum decisions[52]

"I am very afraid to go back to my country because I will have nothing. No place to live, no education, no life."

WAITING TIMES

The Home Office has said that separated children are given priority in the consideration of applications;[53] nonetheless, many still wait a considerable time before receiving a decision. The young people we spoke to had been in England for an average of just over 11 months, yet only 19 of them had received an initial decision on their asylum application. Of these, one under-18 had been refused (on non-compliance grounds), and nine had been granted leave to remain.

Many young people were perplexed by the length of time they had to wait for an asylum decision, especially when people who had arrived more recently than them had received a decision before they had. The stress of waiting for a decision takes its toll on the emotional health of young people

---

[52] It is notable that the Home Secretary has chosen to exclude the Immigration Service from the duties described in the Race Relations (Amendment) Act (2000). The Act outlaws race discrimination and places a general duty on public authorities to be proactive in promoting race equality.

[53] 1993 Immigration rules, HC395 paragraphs 349–52.

already trying to cope with a tremendous amount of change and uncertainty. One 15-year-old described it like this:

> *"I think the Government helps us a lot but people applied* [for asylum] *two years ago, for children it's not good. You gonna go mad with these other things, you shouldn't have to think about this. Have to deal with all these things, you gonna go mad. There should be more focus in children's cases. It's hard. You remain empty. They do whatever they want to you. They can throw you out."*

Lack of information from the Home Office lengthens the time young people have to wait for a decision, and exacerbates their anxiety. For example, one boy had to travel to the Home Office in Croydon once a month to "sign in". He had never been told why. His frustration with this was compounded by the fact that he had to borrow money from a relative in order to fund the trip, as he received no cash or voucher support from social services because he lived in a full-board hostel.

The delays and lack of information also militate against planning for the future. One boy said:

> *"We have been waiting four years* [for an asylum decision]. *How long are they going to make us wait? How can we settle? How can we make plans? We can't without knowing our status. Our lives are always in the air… It is like they are killing us slowly."*

This uncertainty affects service provision as well. Professionals frequently cite it as a reason for failing to plan for the provision of services to young separated asylum-seekers for the long term.

However, the Home Office has recently employed extra staff to work specifically on clearing the backlog of children's claims.

DECISIONS

The Home Office does not produce separate statistics on asylum decisions for separated children. The Refugee Council's Children's Section estimates, on the basis of asylum decisions given to children known to it, that between one and two per cent of young asylum-seekers receive full refugee status. The majority receive exceptional leave to remain (ELR) and a small minority receive a refusal as an initial decision. Many of these refusals are likely to be overturned on appeal as they are due to reasons of non-compliance and the Home Office has said that it will refuse an unaccompanied minor only if it can guarantee it would be able to return them to their home country safely. Clearly, this is difficult to achieve, and so unaccompanied minors are almost never refused after appeal.

However, there are plans to increase efforts to make it easier to return young people when they turn 18 years and to increase the number of returns made in an attempt to "improve our [Home Office] statistics on asylum-seeking children".[54] As a result, ELR is being awarded to young people until their 18th birthday, rather than for the customary four years. A recent Home Office letter stated:

> "*It is IND's* [Immigration and Nationality Directorate's] *policy to seek to enforce the removal of unaccompanied asylum-seeking children who have been refused asylum and who have no other basis of stay in the UK when they reach the age of 18.*"[55]

Given the small proportion of children granted full refugee status, many more separated children could be sent back to their country of origin in the future. This makes it increasingly important that information is gathered to allow immigration officials to fully assess the claims of minors.[56] One professional, a refugee himself, argued that young people could experience particular problems of not being believed by immigration officials:

> "*Usually they don't get believed by the authorities of their stories. And the younger you are, the more suspicions there are around you. You know, if you said, 'I've been a political activist', they would doubt* [you]. *'How come you've become a political activist?'... If I was asked that as a 12-year-old was it possible... to be detained, I would say, 'Most probably he had been detained with his family'... But neither the Home Office nor the court will believe that...*"

The following example shows that there are inconsistencies in the way asylum decisions are made for young separated refugees:

> A social worker reported that a boy in her care had his name taken down incorrectly on his asylum application. At a later date he sought to correct the mistake. As a result he somehow ended up with two asylum applications being considered – one with the wrong name and one with the right name. All the rest of the details were identical. On one application he was granted exceptional leave to remain, on the other he was refused.

Our interviews indicate that young asylum-seekers are very conscious of current Government policy and media sentiment, which focus on being "tough". One boy said:

> "*The Government is getting tight with this problem, they are afraid everyone is coming here.*"

---

[54] Home Office, Asylum and Appeals Policy Directorate Letter, 21 December 2000

[55] Home office letter.

[56] See also Ayotte and Williamson, 2001.

Many emphasised the need to educate citizen people about the circumstances from which they have fled and their desire to make a contribution to the community and not claim benefits.

5.9.4 Family reunification

Although we did not ask the young people about the circumstances which caused them to leave their homes or about where their parents were, some young people brought it up and in particular a number talked about how much they missed their parents:

> *"The main thing is that you are away from your parents… I do feel sad that they're not with me – but it's like – you can't live in the situation – I mean* [on one hand] *I'm* [happy] *that I've escaped from war, and in one situation I'm not happy that my family's not with me."*

Those children who spoke of this also tended to say that they felt it was unfair that they could not be reunited with their parents in the UK. One boy compared the practice to the actions of Saddam Hussein:

> *"It's going to be the same as Saddam Hussein, where he's separating us from our family. It's not going to be much different because if you separate two persons from each other, it's no different, it doesn't matter who does it; the important thing is how the person is going to feel."*

Asylum-seeking children do not automatically have the right to be reunited with their parents or other family members in the UK. The child may apply to the Home Office for their relatives to be allowed to enter the UK on compassionate grounds for the purposes of reunification, but permission will not necessarily be granted (and usually is not).

5.9.5 Detention

It is Government policy not to detain any unaccompanied minor unless in exceptional circumstances, and then for no more than 24 hours, although there are no formal safeguards in place to ensure this does not happen. We spoke to one 17 year old boy who had been held in detention for three months, the reasons for his detention were not clear.

Most detention centres are visited by volunteers, who try to support the detainees. These visitors sometimes refer cases where a person is claiming to be under 18 years to the Refugee Council's Panel of Advisers or the local social services department. The Panel Advisers monitor cases and provide assistance and advocacy where possible but this system does not pick up all cases.

If any detainee claiming to be under 18 is later confirmed to be a child, social services have a responsibility to them, and their needs may be greater as a result of prolonged detention. It is therefore in the interests of social services to work with the immigration service to identify such cases as early as possible. Likewise the immigration service will be keen to ensure the implementation of the government policy on the detention of unaccompanied minors.

Although official figures are not available for the numbers of separated children who are detained, we know that between 1994 and the summer of 2001 the Children's Section at the Refugee Council dealt with almost 250 cases of young people who have been detained; of these the longest detention lasted almost six months.[57]

One local authority asylum team reported that a young refugee had been travelling with a parent who was arrested at Manchester Airport for travelling without correct documentation. The parent had been imprisoned and the child held in a secure unit. The asylum team were co-working with the authority's youth offender team in relation to his care.

---

[57] Personal communication, August 2001.

5.10 Health

Main findings

- Most young separated refugees said they were in good physical health but a significant number appeared to have emotional or, possibly, mental health needs.

- Very few young separated refugees were receiving any kind of emotional or mental health support, due to the lack of availability or accessibility of suitable facilities.

- Young people and professionals alike were concerned about the inability to prepare nutritious food on a very limited budget.

Key factors affecting the health of young people:
- Are they able to access appropriate primary health services?
- Are appropriate mental health services available?

5.10.1 Mental health[58]

"Sometimes I have bad dreams... If I have any problems I just talk with myself."

The emotional or mental health needs of the young people were evident, either directly through their answers to our questions about how they had felt at different times, or indirectly from observation of their responses to more general questions. These issues ranged from feelings of isolation and loneliness to the wish for professional psychiatric treatment.

For example, one boy who was clearly distressed described how he had been thrown against a wall by the Taliban, causing him head injuries. He said he could not sleep at night for thinking about his father and added, "thinking causes diseases in my head". Others felt that their experiences in their country of origin had hardened them to experiences here:

"I have seen much worse in my country, so nothing bad."

---

[58] Many professionals used the expression "mental health issues or needs" when perhaps they were referring to emotional health needs; we use the phrase "emotional or mental health" in order to avoid making implicit judgements on this complex subject.

A common strategy to help them cope was to busy themselves as a distraction from recalling bad experiences they endured in their country of origin or on their journey here:

> *"When I am on my own I get depressed. I start thinking about my family, I start thinking about all the bad things that happen in Afghanistan. I think about the journey over – it was very frightening, I think about being all alone here, nobody really knowing me. I want to be busy then I don't have to think about these things."*

The mental health of young separated refugees was a major concern for many of the adults we interviewed. Many of the teachers we spoke to were very concerned about the "mental health" of their students. Although professionals in all areas remarked on the young people's apparent "maturity", "resilience" and "ability to cope" when compared with their local contemporaries, it is also acknowledged widely that emotional or mental health problems often do not come to the surface until long after a person's arrival in the country. For this reason those working with young separated refugees need to be vigilant.

It was also clear that many teachers had taken on a pastoral role and felt some responsibility for the welfare of their students. However, as we have seen when discussing education (section 5.7), many teachers do not have the opportunity to spend as long as they would like on pastoral support. One teacher described her need to respond to students' isolation:

> *"Some are very, very isolated, they reach out to you as a tutor. You get the feeling that if they couldn't talk to you they would have no one else to talk to… There is a lot of depression… Students don't talk to each other; there is secrecy between them, isolation. We are not aware of the terrible things that have happened to people."*

Two young people attending college said they had found the student support service very useful and support service staff in colleges with large numbers of refugee students reported that these make up a high proportion of their clients.

Despite apparent emotional or mental health needs, very few young people said they were receiving support for these needs. In some cases it is unlikely that they will even request support if they do not feel secure about their entitlement to ask for anything at all. One girl said she felt her social worker should ensure she gets the right kind of help although she did not herself feel confident about her right to ask for things:

> *"As an asylum-seeker I feel I shouldn't say I want this... When I say I want something, I am not demanding it. The social worker should listen to how you feel properly, not just writing all the time… I can't complain, who am I to complain, [I'm] not asking for more help – just the right kind of help."*

Another girl who had received help from social workers clearly felt she had benefited from it emotionally:

> "*They* [social workers] *do help and ask us what we want, everything that they could to make us feel happy, you feel good.*"

Some young people may not ask for help because in their country of origin, emotional or mental health problems are not discussed or are even equated with madness and, as one education professional said, this then makes it difficult to help.

The experience of one college supports the idea that counselling does not appeal to many young refugees. It had contracted professional counsellors, to whom referrals could be made for students with "mental health problems". This is the kind of service advocated by many adults we spoke to. However, the service was cancelled due to lack of take-up and poor feedback by students, including refugee students.

Having said this, it is clear that some young people will in fact benefit from counselling services, as the experience of one boy shows.

After about six weeks in England, one 17-year-old started to have nightmares about what had happened to him in his home country. He went to see his doctor, who prescribed sleeping pills, but they did not stop the dreams. He said:

> "*I felt sad and lonely and start*[ed] *fights with my room-mate.*"

His social worker referred him to the Medical Foundation for the Victims of Torture. He said: "*They* [the Medical Foundation] *are helping me get through it.*"

The Medical Foundation for the Victims of Torture, based in London, was highly regarded by many social workers we spoke to, partly because the professionals there had the necessary specialist knowledge to work with young refugees.

Good practice

An independent counselling service that focuses on the needs of children from minority ethnic backgrounds has been contracted to provide services to those children and young people with less severe mental health needs, and those who are struggling to cope.

A voluntary organisation in another area provides a mental health service to those with more serious needs. The service offers referral to psychiatric specialists at a local hospital for refugee children from two local schools.

Outside London and some areas of the south-east where there are large numbers of refugees, these sorts of specialist counselling services are neither well developed nor widely available, and so there are few opportunities for young refugees to be referred to appropriate mental health services. Indeed, in many areas mental health provision in general – for both refugee and citizen young people – is seriously limited, and this vulnerable group would be among those who would benefit the most from increased provision. One young boy told us he had been waiting to see a psychologist for two years.

A youth worker described the difficulties she had faced in helping a young person to be referred to mental health services and when he eventually was, the service proved inappropriate. The boy had witnessed the murder of his parents and developed a severe physical impediment as a result. The worker had to take him to see a GP seven times before she secured a referral to a specialist. She said:

"Everything took so long and each time he had to tell his story, so that in the end he said, 'Everyone in [city] must know my story now.'"

Several young people told us that they had suffered from headaches, which may have been related to stress. For example, one young person who had visited a doctor in London to complain of bad headaches, said:

"The doctor did not check me, just gave me tablets and more tablets."

She felt this was not the most appropriate treatment. The headaches eventually disappeared when she moved from poor-quality bed-and-breakfast accommodation to a shared house in another area.

In view of the scepticism of some young refugees towards counselling, some individuals and agencies are trying new approaches to addressing emotional or mental health needs. For example, health and social care professionals worked together in the following case to encourage a boy to take up a new activity as an alternative to medical intervention, to help him cope with his depression:

"Last month I was very depressed and I used anti-depression tablets and my doctor told me, 'You need to do some more swimming.' I didn't have enough money to go swimming and I told my social worker and he help me a little bit to be able to go swimming."

> **Good practice**
> A Befriending Project was launched in London in 2000 by the Medical Foundation for Victims of Torture. The project aims to recruit, train and support mentors – from the same country of origin as the separated young people who use their service – to act as advocate and friend to one child for at least two years. The project has encountered some difficulty in recruiting mentors, but the principle had very broad support among the adults we interviewed.

It is crucial that any agency contemplating setting up a mentoring and befriending scheme has vigorous child protection measures in place.

5.10.2 Physical health

Thirty-three of those interviewed were not registered with a GP, and 20 reported problems in getting access to primary health services. All of those in foster care and residential care were registered with a GP, and most of them had also seen a dentist and an optician.

> **Good practice**
> In one London borough a specialist health visitor for "looked after" children has been appointed through Quality Protects to take the lead in developing a health action plan (HAP) for each child. The HAP will record each child's basic details, assess their health needs and ask if these are being met, make referrals where necessary, and ensure they are followed up. The HAP is a collaborative plan worked on by social workers, doctors, carers and the health visitor.

Young people placed "out of area" appeared to have particular difficulty in getting access to health services, despite the fact that private providers are contracted to facilitate access to these services. For example, one boy had to be very persistent to persuade someone to take him to the doctor:

> *"Once I had flu and could not move. I had to ring the agency four times before they would come with a car and take me to the doctor's…They* [the private provider] *wait for days and take us all together on a minibus to save money and time."*

Both social services and health services seemed to have difficulty in dealing with young separated refugees who have particular health needs (see also Albert's case study, page 35). For example, one boy had told social workers that he had problems with his knees but he had been placed in accommodation with several flights of stairs.

One boy aged 17 had suffered a severe injury to his arm in his country of origin. His GP referred him to hospital where was treated for pain for one week. The doctor in the hospital told him he needed to have an operation and he would be sent an appointment date. He had waited six months and had received no further information. Although this may not be unusual it was a source of distress to this boy because he was not aware of the way the health service works and was unable to obtain advice or support. While he waited for an operation the pain from his arm injury meant he could neither study nor work.

Professionals said they often faced problems in delivering healthcare because of their inability to obtain accurate information about numbers of young separated refugees arriving in their area. Although they are notified who is arriving under NASS, they have no information about the numbers or addresses of those refugees who have arrived in the area under other arrangements.

COOKING

"Sometimes when I am short of money, I just eat mayonnaise!" (Boy, aged 17)

The ability of the young people to prepare and cook nutritious food on a limited budget was a cause of concern for a number of adults, and the young people themselves agreed that many of them lacked the skills to prepare nutritious, healthy food. This is of crucial importance for the young people we spoke to who were living independently with no regular adult supervision.

Few young people were confident about their cooking skills as they had never cooked before they came to the UK. Possibly there is an assumption that because young separated refugees have shown great ingenuity and maturity in making the journey to the UK, they must have other life skills to match. This is frequently not the case and some may be suffering from poor nutrition.

Good practice
At a semi-independent hostel run by the Refugee Council for one local authority, staff found that many young people arrived without any cooking skills. They devised a cooking rota where each person (including staff) takes it in turn to cook for everyone else. They are given a budget to do this. This helps develop their budgeting and cooking skills as well as providing the opportunity for everyone to sit down together and get to know each other.

SEXUAL HEALTH

We did not ask young people specifically about sexual health issues and none raised the subject. However, several health professionals raised it as an area in which young separated refugees lacked awareness of the issues.

> **Good practice**
> The Terrence Higgins Trust runs a youth project that takes a broad approach to promoting sexual health. The workers have had some success in holding sessions with young refugees that start off by tackling the subject indirectly. The sessions cover things such as assertiveness, self-esteem, cultural awareness (ie, "you can't do that here") and negotiation skills.

5.11 Conclusion

In the absence of strong leadership from central Government, the level of care and protection received by a young separated refugee arriving in England will vary widely depending on the experience, competence and willingness of local agencies to recognise and meet their needs.

The most important thing we can learn from our interviews with 125 young separated refugees is that they are children first and foremost. Despite their resilience and apparent maturity, young separated refugees deserve and require improvements in the standard of care and the protection they receive – whether they are under or over 16, unaccompanied or accompanied.

6 Recommendations

In Chapter 5 we highlighted examples of good practice and we would recommend the adaptation of any of these examples to local settings. In this chapter we go further and make a series of detailed recommendations which emerge from the findings. The recommendations are arranged according to the agency that should take responsibility for them, and priorities for implementation are highlighted in bold.

Firstly, we present a set of basic principles that should underpin any policy or practice relating to young separated refugees.

Principles of policy

Young separated refugees:
- should be entitled to all the rights enshrined in the UN Convention on the Rights of the Child 1989 and the Children Act (1989)
- are children first and foremost
- are vulnerable and in need of care and protection
- are a potential asset to our society and not a burden.

Central government

- **Government to remove its reservation on applying the UN Convention on the Rights of the Child 1989 to asylum-seeking and other non-citizen children**

Home Office

- **Change the grant paid for the support of young separated refugees so that:**
    - **it meets the reasonable costs of the support of young separated refugees**
    - **it does not distinguish between funds available for under- and over-16-year-olds**
    - **it varies according to local costs**
    - **the amount of the grant is known in advance.**

- **Improve procedures for assessing asylum applications from separated children in order to speed up decision times and ensure fairer decisions.**

- **Do not disperse young separated refugees when they turn 18 and are transferred to NASS.**

- Outlaw the use of X-rays for age-determination purposes.

- Prohibit the detention of possible minors in cases of disputed age.

- Fund the Refugee Council's Panel of Advisers so that they are able to offer services to more children and allocate more time to each child.

- Ensure that young separated refugees have access at the earliest opportunity to an appropriate interpreter who speaks their language.

- Invest in training more immigration officials to specialise in interviewing young separated refugees and working with interpreters.

- Ensure that clear information is given to all young separated refugees about the asylum process, preferably in their first language.

- Monitor the use of non-compliance as a reason given for refusing asylum.

- Ensure that police receive training in asylum and child welfare issues.

Department of Health

- **Specify appropriate forms of care for young separated refugees including strengthening guidance on when Section 20 should be used.**

- **Produce a standard procedure for age determination that involves a holistic approach in which decisions are taken over time.**

- Prohibit the use of local authority-issued vouchers to separated refugee minors and provide cash instead.

- Specifically include the treatment of young separated refugees in the Social Services Inspectorate inspections.

- Consider developing Quality Protects indicators that relate specifically to young separated refugees, and other ways of creating incentives to local authorities to improve services to this group.

Department for Education and Skills

- **Examine the overall package of financial support available through the Ethnic Minority and Traveller Achievement Grant (EMTAG), and the ring-fenced £500 grant.** In particular:
    - Increase the amount available through EMTAG in 2001/2002 to reflect the real cost of integrating refugee students and meeting their needs.
    - Attach the support package to the young person, not the school.
    - Make the grant available in all areas and to separated children being supported by the local authority, as well as all children supported by NASS.

- **Ensure that the National Learning and Skills Council makes the additional needs funding formula flexible enough to take into account the needs of refugees.**

Local government

Social services departments

ARRIVAL, AGE DETERMINATION AND ASSESSMENT

- **Ensure that every child receives a full needs assessment in line with the national framework for assessment.**
  This means:
    - The assessment will lead to action to link the child with other services, such as education and health.
    - Age will not be used as the prime determinant of a child's need.
    - More children will be "looked after" under Section 20 of the Children Act (1989) (including 16- and 17-year-olds).

- Ensure all staff receive training to use the Department of Health's guidelines on the treatment of unaccompanied minors (*Unaccompanied asylum-seeking children. A practice guide and training pack,* 1995) and the UNHCR/International Save the Children Alliance, *Separated Children in Europe Programme: Statement of good practice* (2000, 2nd ed.).

- Ensure that where a child is handed over to the care of a relative, that carer is assessed for their suitability and the placement is supported and monitored, as appropriate.

- Ensure that details of all young separated refugees in their care are passed on to the Panel of Advisers for support on asylum and welfare issues.

ACCOMMODATION

- **Monitor all placements regularly according to statutory obligations, including "out-of-area" and private provider placements.**

- **Provide a range of appropriate accommodation to young separated refugees by:**
    - recruiting a broader range of foster carers from minority ethnic communities/culturally appropriate backgrounds
    - designating a residential home for young separated refugees only, to act as short-term or emergency placement, where appropriate, and avoid the use of other residential homes for the placement of young separated refugees
    - developing a greater range of semi-independent accommodation for young separated refugees.

- **Avoid placements in:**
    - unsupported hostel or bed-and-breakfast accommodation
    - hostels where minors and adults live together unsupervised or where citizen and refugee homeless people live together unsupervised.

- **Ensure all young separated refugees have access to an independent visitors scheme and an independent complaints procedure.**

- Train social workers in asylum issues to enable them to make decisions that are culturally appropriate and ensure the safety of the child.

- Consider local race relations when making placements, especially those "out of area".

- Notify the receiving authority of the arrival of young separated refugees when making "out-of-area" placements, to ensure that local services engage with them and to assist local planning in the receiving area.

SUPPORT FROM SOCIAL WORKERS

- **Ensure that every young separated refugee is allocated a named social worker. If their care is contracted out to a private provider they must – at least – have a contact name and number and information about the social worker's role and how they can help.**

- Ensure that all young separated refugees meet with a social worker on a regular basis; periodically this should be in the young person's accommodation.

- Organise social services so that young separated refugees are the responsibility of specialist workers within children's services.

- Provide welcome/introductory information, in translation, to all new arrivals. Costs could be reduced by joint working with other authorities.

- Include young separated refugees in Quality Protects management action plans, children's services plans and any other relevant strategies.

- Consider funding voluntary organisations to run activity or support groups for young separated refugees.

- Ensure that every young separated refugee has access to a Charter Mark registered legal representative.

- Ensure that all young separated refugees are accompanied to asylum screening interviews and that the accompanying adults are fully informed about asylum procedures and child welfare issues.

- Ensure that every young separated refugees is registered with a GP.

- Ensure that training is given in independent living skills such as cooking and budgeting.

FINANCIAL SUPPORT

- **Provide cash financial support to all young separated refugees supported under Section 17, including those in full-board accommodation and those currently receiving local authority vouchers.**

- Inform all young separated refugees of their financial entitlements and apply these entitlements consistently. Social workers should retain some discretion to make additional one-off payments where necessary.

- Consider the location where a young person is living and educational costs when determining how much financial support to provide (eg, those living in rural areas require additional funds for transport).

TRANSITION AT 18 YEARS

- Ensure there are clear procedures for young separated asylum-seekers to continue receiving appropriate support if they are granted leave to remain, and after they reach the age of 18. Provide young people with information about these procedures.

Environmental services

- Work with social services and landlords to vigorously enforce minimum standards.

- Guarantee a prompt response time to complaints from separated children.

Local education authorities

- Ensure that resources are available to address the specific needs of young separated refugees in relation to learning opportunities and to maximise those opportunities through one or more of the following:
  - Develop a flexible floating support service or fast response team through EMTAG, which is available to all schools to help them cope with an influx of new refugee children in their classes. This may require an assessment of the costs and benefits of the devolution of the EMTAG to schools.
  - Make a greater LEA commitment to match-fund the EMTAG so that there are sufficient teachers available to service those schools which need extra support.
  - Ensure that the assessment facility provided through the grant is fully used by schools.
  - Recruit refugee education support teachers, to identify educational needs and help young people receive appropriate education, and provide in-class and homework support (this could be done in co-operation with social services through Quality Protects).

- Work with schools and colleges to ensure that refugee students can get adequate pastoral support through support services and Connexions advisers.

- Provide guidelines and support for schools inexperienced in coping with the needs of refugee children.

Schools and colleges

- Ensure that young separated refugees have opportunities to mix with non-refugee students.

- Incorporate the training of teachers in asylum issues and approaches to tackling racist bullying in all anti-bullying strategies.

- Provide appropriate post-16 courses in the 6th Form if there are significant numbers of young separated refugees in a school.

- Link up with volunteer groups to provide homework support to young separated refugees (ensuring that all volunteers are police-checked).

- Target young separated refugees through the Connexions service to help them maximise their educational opportunities and set realistic targets.

- Develop college programmes that include English as a Second or Other Language (ESOL), A/AS levels, GCSE, vocational and taster courses and training in independent living skills through support from the local learning and skills councils.

Youth and leisure services

- Consider ways to make leisure facilities more accessible to young separated refugees; for example, by giving them a card that provides free access or designating a particular time and place for use by them.

- Carry out preventive interventions with young separated refugees through the youth offending teams.

Health authorities and primary care trusts

- Provide training to GPs in the circumstances and health needs of young separated refugees and provide them with information about appropriate points of referral.

- Increase the provision of and access to a range of mental health services for young separated refugees.

- Ensure there are staff available to address the specific needs of young separated refugees (eg, specialist health visitor or primary care facilitator).

- Promote the use of health action plans for "looked after" young separated refugees.

- Develop projects to promote the sexual health of young separated refugees

Inter-agency action

Produce inter-agency strategies on supporting young separated refugees and establish monitoring groups to guide and ensure the implementation of the strategies. Statutory and voluntary agencies should participate in the strategy. The strategy should include the following actions:

- Develop a database of young separated refugees in the area for the purpose of grant applications and planning service delivery.

- Improve inter-agency information-sharing and communication.

- Social services and education department to develop the use of personal education plans for all "looked after" young separated refugees.

- Social services and education department to ensure that all young separated refugees are aware of and able to benefit from their entitlement to free school meals.

- Social services and the Immigration Service to monitor detention centres for the presence of minors and develop procedures for ensuring the swift release of young separated refugees.

- Health services and voluntary organisations to explore different approaches to addressing the emotional and/or mental health needs of young separated refugees including social activities and befriending schemes.

- Consider ways to develop work with voluntary organisations including refugee community organisations.

Voluntary agencies

- **Refugee community organisations and other voluntary organisations should promote positive images of refugees to make young separated refugees feel proud of their heritage and counter negative public perceptions.**

- Develop tailored support for young separated refugees through refugee community organisations. For example, set up activity groups aimed at young people and in particular look at the need for groups aimed specifically at girls.

Appendix 1: Glossary of terms

Separated: "Children under 18 years of age who are outside their country of origin and separated from both parents or their legal/customary primary care giver" (United Nations High Commissioner for Refugees and Save the Children, *Separated Children in Europe Programme: Statement of good practice,* 1995 para. 2.1). We use the term "separated" in this report to refer both to children who are unaccompanied and to those who are accompanied (see below).

Unaccompanied: Children under 18 years of age who are outside their country of origin and *not* accompanied by a close relative.

Accompanied: Children under 18 years of age who are outside their country of origin and accompanied by an adult who is *not* their parent or legal/customary care-giver. The adult is not necessarily able, suitable or willing to care for the child. The adult may be an uncle, cousin, sibling or a non-blood relation with whom they have some relationship, such as being from the same village.

Asylum-seeker: A person who has applied for asylum in the UK and has not received a final decision on their application.

Refugee: A person who has applied for asylum and met the Refugee Convention criteria (see below), and been awarded full refugee status. This ordinarily entitles them to remain in the UK indefinitely. We use the term "refugee" to include those seeking refugee status, ie, asylum-seekers, unless it is important to specify immigration status.

The United Nations Convention on Refugees (1951) defines a refugee as someone who has "a well-founded fear of persecution due to race, religion, nationality, political opinion or membership of a political group".

ELR (Exceptional Leave to Remain) and ILR (Indefinite Leave to Remain): ELR is the status granted to a person who has not met the Refugee Convention criteria, but who is allowed to stay in the UK for a definitive period for other reasons – such as, it would be dangerous for them to return to their country of origin. Those with ELR may apply for settlement/ILR after four years.

Appendix 2: Summary of young separated refugees project initiatives

Pilot initiatives are being set up across England, in partnership with statutory and voluntary agencies, to meet some of the needs identified in this research with young separated refugees. The initiatives have been funded for between 12 and 18 months starting from July 2001. A practice-based guide on working with young separated refugees will be prepared in 2003 following evaluation of the various initiatives. Brief descriptions of the initiatives that have been approved to date are given below.

Young Person's Adviser at Heathrow Airport

A Young Person's Adviser has been appointed to support young unaccompanied minors through the reception process at Heathrow Airport. The post has been created with match funding from the European Refugee Fund. The Adviser will be based and managed by Refugee Arrivals Project (RAP), one of the largest voluntary organisations working with refugees. The Adviser will also provide training and guidance to personnel working with unaccompanied minors at ports of entry in the south-east to help promote appropriate policies and procedures.

Young Women Asylum-Seekers Project, west London

This project aims to provide a support network for isolated young women (aged between 13 and 18 years) in the west London area. The project is being run by the Portobello Trust's Youth Enterprise Scheme in partnership with a west London social services department. Activities planned for the group include: vocational training; drama and art work; developing a peer support group to address housing, education, training and employment needs; and the opportunity to undertake voluntary work. The aims of the project are to develop the young women's skills; increase interaction within the local community; boost confidence and improve self-esteem; and, above all, to have some fun!

Young Refugee Rights Project, west London

This is a project run by and for young refugees in west London. Its aims include: informing young separated refugees about their rights; providing information about services and support available locally; and challenging prejudice and promoting understanding of issues facing young separated refugees. The project is supported by Save the Children's London Development Team.

Mental Health Resource Project, Hull

This project is run by the Tuke Centre, part of a psychiatric hospital, involved in supporting services for the mental health of refugees since 1995. The project will provide training and consultations to statutory agencies in Hull, such as social services and primary healthcare services, to enable them to carry out sensitive needs assessments of young separated refugees, and improve professionals' understanding of the impact of loss and trauma.

Connexions Project, West Midlands

This initiative is run by Coventry and Warwickshire Connexions. The Connexions service allocates young people a personal adviser to help them to maximise their educational opportunities and also provide advice and support in other aspects of young people's lives so as to remove barriers to learning. In Coventry and Warwickshire seven personal advisers will be allocated to work specifically with young refugees in the area, and over 100 more will be given training on the particular issues facing young refugees to help them support this group.

Young Separated Refugees Support Worker, Newcastle

Newcastle Social Services are recruiting a worker to support young separated refugees in the area. The support worker will help young people get access to education and training opportunities, health services and local leisure facilities and will provide individual casework for those who have particular problems with, for example, housing. The worker will also assist the young people to meet as a group and will organise social activities. A multi-agency advisory group will guide and support the worker in their role.

Youth Mentoring Project, Oxford

Oxfordshire Youth Service in partnership with a local voluntary organisation, Asylum Welcome, are establishing a team of volunteer mentors from the local community, including the refugee community, to support young separated refugees in Oxford. The mentors will support young people who have particular difficulties through a period of immense change in their lives. Mentors will help young people to live independently and to make use of services available to them.

Bibliography and further reading

1. Association of Chief Police Officers, *ACPO Guide to Meeting the Policing Needs of Asylum-Seekers and Refugees*, ACPO, 2001

2. Audit Commission, *Another Country: Implementing dispersal under the Immigration and Asylum Act 1999*, Audit Commission, 2000

3. W Ayotte, *Supporting Unaccompanied Children in the Asylum Process*, Save the Children, 1998

4. W Ayotte and L Williamson, *Separated Children in the UK: An overview of the current situation*, Save the Children and Refugee Council, 2001

5. M Candappa and I Egharevba, 'Extraordinary Childhoods: The social lives of refugee children', in *Children 5–16 Research Briefing*, Economic and Social Research Council, 2000

6. Children's Consortium, *Briefing on education and refugee children*, 2000

7. A Dawson, *Monocultural Communities and their Affect on Asylum/Immigration Seekers in Humberside*, Save the Children, 2001

8. Department of Health, Department for Education and Employment, Home Office, *Framework for the Assessment of Children in Need and their Families*, The Stationery Office, 2000

9. Department of Health, *Children (Leaving Care) Act (2000) guidance*, 2001

10. Department of Health, *The UK's First Report to the UN Committee on the Rights of the Child*, 1994

11. Department of Health, *Social Services Performance in 1999-2000*

12. Directorate of Public Health, The Health of Londoners Project, *Refugee Health in London*, 1999

13. S Drew, *Children and the Human Rights Act*, Save the Children, 2000

14. D Garvie, *Far From Home: The housing of asylum seekers in private-rented accommodation*, Shelter, 2001

15. Home Office, *Asylum and Appeals Policy Directorate Letter*, 21 December 2000

16. Home Office, *Full and Equal Citizens: A strategy for the integration of refugees into the United Kingdom*, 2001

17. Home Office, Research and Development Statistics Direcotrate, *Asylum Statistics UK 2000*, 25th September 2001

18. Horn of Africa Youth Scheme, *Let's Spell it Out*, Save the Children, 1998

19. R Kohli, 'Breaking the silence', in *Professional Social Work Journal*, June 2000

20. E Little, 'Children First and Foremost', in *Community Care*, 18-24 January 2001

21. G Mott, *Refugees and Asylum-Seekers: The role of the LEAs*, 2001

22. N Munoz, *Other People's Children*, Children of the Storm and London Guildhall University, 2000

23. National Asylum Support Service, *Draft Education - Policy Bulletin 63*, 30th August 2001

24. National Asylum Support Service, *Policy Bulletin 29: Transition at 18*, 6th October 2000

25. National Council of Voluntary Child Care Organisations, *Briefing: Connexions*, NCVCCO, January 2001

26. Refugee Council, *Refugee Council Briefing: Support for unaccompanied refugee children turning 18?*, Refugee Council, March 2001

27. Refugee Council, *Refugee Council Briefing: The Immigration and Asylum Act 1999*, Refugee Council, January 2000

28. Royal College of Paediatricians and Child Health, *The Health of Refugee Children: Guidelines for paediatricians*, Kings Fund, 1999

29. S Russell, *Most Vulnerable of All: The treatment of unaccompanied children in the UK*, Amnesty International, 1999

30. J Rutter and C Jones, *Refugee Education: Mapping the field*, Trentham Books, 1998

31. T Smith, 'A Refuge for Children? The Impact of the Immigration and Asylum Act', *Poverty Journal*, No 105, 2000

32. Social Services Inspectorate, *Unaccompanied Asylum-Seeking Children: A practice guide and training pack*, Department of Health, 1995

33. R Stone, *Children First and Foremost: Meeting the needs of unaccompanied, asylum-seeking children*, Barnado's, 2000

34. United Nations High Commission for Refugees/Save the Children, *Separated Children in Europe Programme: Statement of good practice,* UNHCR/Save the Children, 2000 (2nd ed)

35. G Younge, 'The Waiting Game', *The Guardian (G2),* 22 May 2001

36. www.legislation.hmso.gov.uk, *The Children Act 1989: Guidance and regulations*

37. www.legislation.hmso.gov.uk, *The Children (Leaving Care) Act 2000*

38. www.legislation.hmso.gov.uk, *The Immigration Appeals (Procedure) (Amendment) Rules 1993*

Regional reports on young separated refugees

Young separated refugees in Greater Manchester by Dr Edward Mynott and Dr Beth Humphries. For further information contact Miranda Kaunang at m.kaunang@scfuk.org.uk or 0161 434 8337

Young separated refugees in Hillingdon by Kate Stanley. For further information contact Elli Free at e.free@scfuk.org.uk or 020 8741 4054 ext.124

Young separated refugees in Oxford by Kate Stanley. For further information contact Maria Cross at m.cross@scfuk.org.uk or 01865 792 662

Young separated refugees in Newcastle by Clive Hedges, Andrew Render and Kate Stanley. For further information contact Andrew Render at a.render@scfuk.org.uk or 0191 222 1816

Young separated refugees in the West Midlands by Katherine Marriott. For further information contact Katherine Marriott at k.marriott@scfuk.org.uk or 0121 555 8888

Young separated refugees in Yorkshire and Humberside by Dr Andrew Dawson and Sarah Holding. For further information contact Michelle Foster at m.foster@scfuk.org.uk or 0113 242 4844

Young separated refugees in [a London borough] by Kate Stanley.